Olusegun Adeniyi

❈

NAKED
ABUSE

SEX FOR GRADES IN AFRICAN UNIVERSITIES

Foreword by
Bisi Adeleye-Fayemi

Plus
Insights from the Ife Webinar on 'Finding Safe Spaces
for Female Students in Nigerian Universities'

Cover design by Sunny Hughes 'Sunza'

CONTENTS

CONTENTS

CONTENTS

DEDICATION

To the cherished memories of my friend, Pius Adebola Adesanmi and my brother, Agboola

ACKNOWLEDGEMENT

The idea for this book came in the course of a conversation with the Director, West African Office, Ford Foundation, Mr Innocent Chukwuma, who believes that sexual harassment on the campuses of institutions of higher learning is a serious social menace that must be tackled. Chukwuma threw the challenge at me with the pledge of a grant from Ford Foundation if I could research the issue and he was true to his word. My appreciation also goes to Ms Nancy Scally of the Ford Foundation' Institute of International Education.

However, this current edition has benefitted from the insights and assistance provided by several people, including the Vice Chancellor of the Obafemi Awolowo University (OAU), Ile-Ife, Prof Eyitope Ogunbodede, who hosted a Webinar to discuss how to create safe space for female students in Nigerian universities. The presentations at the session come as Part Two in this edition. I thank Vice President Yemi Osinbajo, SAN, GCON, and the Deputy Senate President, Ovie Omo-Agege who attended the Webinar and shared their perspectives on how to tackle the challenge. I am also grateful to HRH Muhammadu Sanusi II, the 14th Emir of Kano, Professor Joy Ngozi Ezeilo of the University of Nigeria,

Nsukka, Hajiya Saudatu Mahdi, Secretary General of the Women's Rights Advancement and Protection Alternative (WRAPA) as well as Professors Oluyemisi Obilade and Funmi Soetan of OAU who drove the Webinar. I must also thank the OAU acting Director, Centre for the Gender and Social Policy Studies, Dr Monica Orisadare and Head of the ICT unit, Mr Kanmi Adewara. The duo worked tirelessly with me to make the Webinar a success.

Tremendous support for this project also came from the Minister of Education, Mallam Adamu Adamu and the Independent Corrupt Practices Commission (ICPC) Chairman, Prof Bolaji Owasanoye, both of whom asked their officials to provide whatever information I needed for this book. I am particularly grateful to the ICPC Director of Legal Department, Mr Adenekan Shogunle as well as former Chairman of the Commission, Mr Ekpo Nta, who currently chairs the National Salaries, Income and Wages Commission (NSIWC). I must also thank the Executive Secretary of the National Universities Commission (NUC) Prof. Abubakar Rasheed and the Permanent Secretary, Federal Ministry of Education, Mr Sonny Echono for their support. Ms Jackie Farris, the Director General of the Shehu Musa Yar'Adua Centre and Dr Chidi Amuta, read the first draft and made helpful suggestions; and so did the First Lady of Ekiti State, Mrs Bisi Adeleye-Fayemi who wrote the Foreword and also participated at the Ife Webinar. I owe a big debt of gratitude to Dr Abimbola Adelakun, Assistant Professor of African and African Diaspora Studies at the University of Texas at Austin. Her suggestions were invaluable. Same with Ms Ayisha Osori, Executive Director of the Open Society Initiative for West Africa (OSIWA), whose insights helped me to avoid some potentially tragic pitfalls.

My appreciation also goes to Mr Ibraheem Sanusi, an

Advisor on the Joint African Union–German Cooperation on Citizens Participation and Innovative Data Use who explored his contacts across the continent by helping to reach out to the following: Dr Melvis Ndiloseh, a senior lecturer and policy analyst in Cameroon; Ms Nancy Muigei, a governance expert in Kenya; and Nebila Abdulmelik, a Pan-African and feminist writer from Ethiopia. I am grateful to my Ugandan friend, Mr Asavia Philip Nampandu through whom I was able to access Ms Dianah Ahumuza, a lecturer at the School of Law, Makerere University.

I must also express my profound appreciation to the Executive Director of Gender Mobile Initiative, Ms. Omowumi Ogunrotimi, and my brother, JJ Omojuwa who offered tremendous assistance in the course of researching this book. Also of immeasurable assistance, especially in the area of research, were Mr Peter Ishaka and Dr Monday Ekpe as well as Dipo Akinkugbe, Perkins Abaje, Olusesan Adeniyi, Sunny Hughes, Loveth Owunezi and Tunde Ahmadu. Transportation Minister, Mr Chibuike Rotimi Amaechi and the Independent National Electoral Commission (INEC) Chairman, Prof Mahmud Yakubu were also very helpful. And so were my ever dependable friends: Waziri Adio, Ola Awoniyi, Emeka Ihedioha, Mustapha Dennis Onoyiveta, Amara Nwankpa, Wale Banmore, Ifeoma Ngozi Malo, Simon Kolawole, Bolaji Abdullahi and Kingsley Obiora.

Very special thanks to the Chairman of Caverton Group, Mr Remi Makanjuola who was particularly instrumental to the publication of this book. I am immensely grateful for his uncommon generousity. I am also grateful to Senator Daisy Danjuma for her assistance. To everyone at THISDAY, from our Chairman, Mr Nduka Obaigbena, who encourages me, to other colleagues, I am also appreciative. Right from the beginning of this project, Dr Kole Shettima, the MacArthur

Foundation Director for Africa Office, who has been both an adviser and a supportive mentor, not only showed interest, he offered useful suggestions all through.

Given how important this work is to me, I had no hesitation in reaching out to my sister, Ms Molara Wood once again. And I cannot thank her enough for editing this book at very short notice. I must also thank Professor Jacob K. Olupona, Chair of the Committee on African Studies at the Harvard Divinity School and Dr Samuel Oloruntoba, a lecturer at the Thabo Mbeki African Leadership Institute, University of South Africa for their kind support.

Writing this book at a time when my two daughters are university students has meant that I had to seek their views, and they both provided interesting insights. Toluwani, in Beijing, shared with me how the Chinese deal with such issues - while Ifeoluwa, in Amherst, MA, explained the protections offered female students in the United States. I thank them both as I do my wife, Oluwatosin and son, Oluwakorede, for their love and encouragement. But in the end, the glory for the successful completion of this project belongs to our Lord Jesus Christ.

FOREWORD

When I was a student at the then University of Ife (now Obafemi Awolowo University) in the 1980s, there was a story about a female student in the Pharmacy Department, a few years before our time. This student had been propositioned by one of her lecturers and she turned him down. At the end of the semester, she failed his course. Quite naturally, she repeated the course. But she failed again. When she went to check her results for the third time, after spending almost two additional years working towards her degree, she went berserk. On realizing that she had failed again, she started unbuttoning her blouse and yelling at the top of her voice, '*Dr XYZY, se o fe se mi? Oya, wa se!*', ('Dr XYZY, do you want to have sex with me? Come on, let's do it now!')

Hysterical, the poor girl started walking down the stairs towards the lecturer's office, stripping as she went, before other female students gathered to restrain her. The university authorities waded in and the student graduated eventually. But nothing happened to Dr XYZY. That part of the story did not come as a surprise. After abusing his authority and driving his student literally insane, there ought to have been consequences for him. Wishful thinking. Things did not work that way then, and it seems nothing much has changed.

In my third year, I registered for a course in my department. A day after the first class on this course, I took a document to my lecturer to sign. He made a pass at me, and when I refused, he said he would wait and see if I would change my mind, after all I had just started the course. Not sure if what I had heard was a joke, a veiled threat or both, I mentioned my concerns to another friend who was in the same department but not taking his course. She told me there were stories about the man. After registration, you had up to two weeks to change your mind and register elsewhere. The next day I withdrew my registration from his class. When I was in postgraduate school, another lecturer tried the same thing. I reported him to my thesis supervisor who had a quiet word with him. Of course he denied the harassment, claiming he had only been joking with me. He however got the message and backed off.

In October 2019, I attended the screening of the BBC Documentary, 'Sex for Grades', at the Sheraton Hotel in Lagos. I could not believe what I was watching. I laughed at the pitiful sight of a grown man bumping and grinding in front of a girl young enough to be his daughter, claiming to be praying for her. I cried when it turned out that the brave young woman who produced the documentary, Kiki Mordi, had to drop out of university on account of the sexual harassment she faced. I sat with my mouth open at the sight of 'The Cold Room', where young female students were taken to be 'frozen' by their lecturers. I was angry at the lack of respect for the young women and the absence of any sense of decorum by the male predators. However, I was also pleased that the dreadful culture of silence about sexual harassment in our higher institutions was finally being broken.

I was therefore delighted when my good friend and brother, Olusegun Adeniyi, asked me to write the foreword to this book, 'Naked Abuse: Sex for Grades in African Universities', which is a concise study of sexual harassment in tertiary institutions across the African continent. The author is a well-respected public intellectual, a brilliant analyst, and a thoughtful writer who has meticulously borne witness to some of our most critical moments as a nation. Sexual harassment is one of those insidious practices that continues to go unchecked and is quite frankly not taken seriously. As stated in the introduction to this carefully researched book, sexual harassment in higher institutions is a global issue.

Considering the lack of policy frameworks, inadequate or non-existent procedures, the dearth of support systems, and zero political will to drive these issues, a culture of impunity is rife in most African tertiary institutions. Adeniyi paints a painfully true picture of the state of affairs in these institutions from one country to another. Starting with several disturbing case studies in Nigeria, and on to 29 other countries spread across all the regions of the continent, a clear pattern emerges. The pattern tells us that many male lecturers all over, have a sense of entitlement to the bodies of their female students.

These male teachers have enormous power over their students, and they use that power to threaten, cajole, obstruct justice, collude, persuade and reward. It is therefore extremely difficult for allegations of sexual harassment or misconduct to stick. Many university authorities quickly close ranks to protect the image of the institution. Predators do not operate in isolation; they are part of a culture that indulges in, and encourages preying on vulnerable students.

Young female students attend tertiary institutions to receive an education. They look up to their teachers, male and female alike, for guidance and mentoring, all of which require trust. The female students likely see a big brother type or a father figure. More often than not, their teachers see hot young bodies that are available for the asking or taking.

There is a worrisome narrative in the last chapter, 'The Other Side of the Coin', concerning the increase in the number of female students who themselves are aggressors and do all they can to lure their lecturers into sexual relationships for marks. There are sadly many of such cases, and the author is right to point this out because a number of male lecturers keep repeating this like some kind of mantra. This does not change the main narrative, which is the accountability of adult teachers and the duty they owe those who are placed in their care to learn. It's not unusual that some young girls will have crushes on their teachers, and there are always the lazy ones who would rather play around than study.

Faced with the prospect of failure, they resort to seeking 'Sexually Transmitted Grades', a phrase the author picked up from his research in Gabon. When this happens, the onus is on the adults concerned, who are entrusted with a sacred responsibility, to say no. It is an abuse of power and breach of trust for teachers to take advantage of impressionable young girls. That said, the fact remains that the vast majority of victims of sexual harassment are those who have unwanted attention forced upon them, the 'naughty' ones are a minority.

For Adeniyi to take the time to address the issue of sexual harassment this diligently is a huge contribution to knowledge and public awareness, which will hopefully inspire further action. Sadly, patriarchal oppression works in many ways. Silencing is one of them. African feminists have lent their insights and experiences to the issue of sexual harassment and sexual violence for a long time. One of the ways in which we can see traction on this agenda is to broaden the audience as much as possible, and at the same time encourage as many voices as we can, both male and female.

In adding his voice to this topic, Olusegun Adeniyi is on the right side of history, as he has always been. No society can make progress if it treats 50 per cent of its population with disdain. If young girls are unable to acquire an education in a safe environment and in peace, and go into the world to be the best they can, we will never achieve the development we seek. If our daughters have to spend their time in university dodging the erections and desperate clutches of teachers who are supposed to be their role models, then it should be no surprise if we end up with generations of physically and emotionally scarred women who are unproductive and dependent. Where there are laws and policies in place to prevent and deal with sexual harassment, they should be implemented to the full.

Every tertiary institution needs a policy on sexual harassment and a zero tolerance culture. The leadership of tertiary institutions need to demonstrate that they are serious about the issue and will not condone a culture of abuse, silence and impunity. Women's organisations that are working to provide support for young women to deal with these issues, need to be encouraged. I hope this book is read and used widely for advocacy and capacity building. Thank you, Olusegun Adeniyi, for a job very well done. You have given a lot of food for thought, and as the young people say these days, you have 'shaken a lot of tables'.

Bisi Adeleye-Fayemi
Ado-Ekiti, Ekiti State
12th January 2020

INTRODUCTION

Tertiary institutions are designed to achieve exalted objectives. They, especially universities, are expected to be platforms for the exchange of ideas, centres for advanced learning and producers of genuine graduates in various disciplines upon whose shoulders rests the progress of societies. Put simply, the world should be able to count on these institutions to train and nurture minds that would carry on the tasks of social, economic and political engineering and more. The validation of those ideals, however, requires the presence of key variables such as willing and committed learners, as well as devoted and competent teachers who will not abuse their trust.

In the university system, as in other educational or vocational institutions, interactions between teachers and their students are inevitable, notwithstanding the mode of instruction and assessment. The learner looks up to the lecturer for knowledge and at some point, the latter would have to decide the proficiency of the former through examinations. In sane environments, that exercise can be trusted to be routine and professional. Unfortunately, the student-teacher relationship has become an instrument for unwholesome practices on university campuses across the continent. For sure, the malaise of male lecturers demanding sexual gratification from female students is not exclusive to Africa; it is a global problem. The challenge on the continent is that because the authorities are in denial, many university campuses are increasingly becoming unsafe for female students. The fear of failing and dropping out of school is pushing some of them to accept solicitations that reduce them and their self-worth.

That there is a notable lack of political will to address this malaise could be glimpsed from the manner the 'Sexual Harassment in Tertiary Education Institution: Prohibition Bill, 2016' was handled in Nigeria. Proposed by Senator Ovie Omo-Agege, (current Deputy Senate President), the bill was initially rejected by the 8th National Assembly in deference to the opposition by the Academic Staff Union of Universities (ASUU). But the current Senate has passed the bill and is now awaiting the concurrence of the House of Representatives.

Speaking at a Senate public hearing on the bill in 2018, ASUU President, Prof. Biodun Ogunyemi, argued that sexual harassment is a societal problem and to that extent, it was wrong to target lecturers. "The bill is discriminatory, selective, spiteful, impulsive and lacks logic," said Ogunyemi, who told the lawmakers that "sexual harassment takes place everywhere, including the National Assembly," while arguing that the whole idea was against the spirit of university autonomy.[1]

In a society where people in positions of authority have tended to believe 'nothing goes for nothing,' ASUU's point that transactional sex is not restricted to the campuses is quite valid. But the lecturers miss the real point. While we agree that the challenge is first and foremost a reflection of the moral anomy in our society, the prevailing culture of silence within institutions of higher learning has enabled abusers to act as though above the law. It is the same in most universities across the continent.

However, there is a counter to the whole argument about sex for grades. A former National Universities Commission (NUC) Executive Secretary, Professor Peter Okebukola, believes that any attempt to tackle the problem must also examine the other side. "All those girls who run after lecturers or can be harassed by lecturers are those who are academically weak," he said. "Even, if the lecturers do not want to get engaged with them sexually, the girls will offer them their bodies."

Okebukola is not alone in this thinking. "There is also a growing trend of female students harassing or seducing their male lecturers for better grades, or other reasons, of which little is known... Such female students are reported to go to the extent of offering to pay for hotel rooms for their male lecturers to have sex with them in exchange for good grades," stated a detailed report on the issue.[2]

While there is some truth in the assertion that there are female students who lure lecturers for sex in exchange for grades, it still does not address the issue of public trust. A person occupying a superior position of power cannot use it as an instrument of exploitation, blackmail, coercion, intimidation or implicit threat as is often the case on many of our campuses. While the social dysfunction that encourages this misconduct on university campuses may be an aspect of the larger problem of corruption, there should be no place for sexual predation in an environment of learning.

In describing sex for grades as a serious form of corruption in which sex rather than money is the currency of the bribe at the Ife Webinar, Vice President Osinbajo said interrogating how to create safe spaces for female students in our universities must begin from the question: 'Why is it that an evidently rampant wrongdoing is so under-reported?'. The answer, Osinbajo added, can be located in "the fact that many victims do not feel confident that they will get redress, or that they will be treated fairly or that they will end up suffering the same consequences the predator had threatened would occur if they did not submit to their demands. Then there is, of course, the shame and stigma that could attend speaking up."

Both Nigeria's Education Minister, Mallam Adamu Adamu, who said the issue would be tackled head-on, and Kenyan governance expert, Ms Nancy Muigei, agree with Osinbajo that we cannot de-link corruption from the sex for grades phenomenon. "In many parts of Africa, it's socially acceptable behaviour to give bribes in order to get a service, due to poor service delivery. How different is this from a student being coerced to buy grades in exchange for sex? Perhaps it's time we opened the debate further, to understand why this has persisted and how we can craft lasting solutions especially touching on the quality of education and its relevance," Muigei said.

While acknowledging that this is likely to happen whenever power is threatened and the status quo is challenged, Nebila Abdulmelik, a Pan-Africanist and feminist writer from Ethiopia, argues that the most worrisome aspect of the menace is, "The silencing or muting of those who speak truth to power. These voices and stories deserve to be told and retold, to be heard and, beyond that, to influence and shape policies and practices at all levels." The sordid practice, according to Abdulmelik, has become too pervasive that, "Unless we do something about it in our spheres of influence and using the tools we have at our disposal, including shifting regressive socio-cultural and gender norms, the problem will not go away."

This is representative of the views of several academics and civil society activists that I spoke to across Africa about this menace. On the whole, the essence of this intervention is to start a conversation around institutionalized practices that rig the educational system against women and undermine the credibility of their qualifications. But, aside looking at the issue of sexual harassment of female students by male lecturers, a chapter in this book also examines 'the other side' without making excuses for the crime. For reforms to happen, it is crucial that we acknowledge all sides to this debate. If women are treated only as passive victims all the time, we will end up making only lopsided laws that will not get to the core of the issue.

In writing this book, therefore, my main objectives include: raising the profile of discourse on sexual harassment in tertiary institutions on the continent, deepening awareness of the drivers, risks and consequences of the culture of gender-based violence on our campuses, and influencing the development and implementation of policies and systems to tackle the challenge. Exposing the culture of sex-for-marks, I believe, would not only help highlight the malaise, it could also kick- start efforts towards curbing predatory behaviour on our campuses. Only then can we truly begin to make education spaces safe for women and girls in Africa.

Olusegun Adeniyi
Abuja, 16th September 2020

ENDNOTES

1 https://thenationonlineng.net/asuu-kicks-senate-sexual-harassment-bill/
2 https://ogalecturer.com/concern-rises-over-sexual-harassment-on-ni- geri an-campuses/

Those of us women of a certain age, retired now, have dealt with these behaviors across decades for our entire careers. We had no one to turn to when our professors, supervisors, and colleagues made raucous comments, touched us without permission, or pushed themselves up against us in hallways, offices, and classrooms. Sexual impropriety among men towards working women and students was, and is still, pervasive. The difference? Women are speaking up because people are finally listening, and now it's the men who are guarded. I say, it's about time!

– LOVETOBIRD, STONYBROOK, NY

CHAPTER ONE

A TALE OF TWO
NIGERIAN PROFESSORS

For decades, female students in Nigerian universities have been tormented by male lecturers who demand sexual gratification in return for grades. And while definitive statistics may not be readily available in order to determine how many have been abused, there is no doubt that the number is high. Very few victims can muster the reserves of strength to suffer the often grave consequences of telling their stories. So the majority keep silent, seeing no option but to try to graduate without adding insult to injury. But with conversations and other interactions increasingly being recorded, lecherous lecturers are being caught red-handed by smart female students who now have the tools to turn the tables against them.

Education Minister, Mallam Adamu Adamu who said the sexual harassment of students by lecturers has gone on for far too long, described it as "the worst form of corruption" in our country because of its implications on the future of our girls and women. "No system should tolerate the kind of abuse that is now prevalent on the campuses and we are going to combat it," vowed Adamu, who gathered senior officials in his ministry including Permanent Secretary, Mr Sonny Echono, to share with me some of the policy options being considered to deal with the menace.

LITANY OF SHAME

In September 2014, a lecturer at the Ahmadu Bello University (ABU), Zaria, sneaked into a hostel, disguised as a woman and wearing a hijab, to meet a female student with whom he was having an inappropriate relationship[1]. In 2012, a seven-minute video of a sexual harassment conversation between an Engineering lecturer at Ambrose Alli University, Ekpoma and a female student, went viral[2]. At Lagos State University (LASU), Ojo, in 2005, a lecturer was caught in his underpants in a hotel room with a 200-level female undergraduate he was exploiting[3]. In August 2016, a 400-level student of the Department of Languages and Linguistics at Osun State University released a 30-minute video clip of an encounter with one of her lecturers in a hotel room[4]. In the video, the female student set up a laptop directly opposite the bed and pretended to be watching 'Things Fall Apart'[5] while the stark naked lecturer caressed her, unaware that he was being captured on film. In May 2016, an audio clip of the head of the Department of English, University of Ilorin, sexually harassing one of his students, went viral[6]. His victim, said to be a 200-level student of the department, had gone to the lecturer's office concerning a continuous assessment test she had missed, and he seized the opportunity to solicit for sex, not knowing that she was recording him. In shame, the lecturer tendered his letter of resignation from the university.[7]

Given the prevailing culture of bad behaviour, there are just too many examples to cite. The situation is not helped by the disposition of university authorities that are more concerned about the image of their institutions than the plight of their students, leading to many predatory lecturers seeing themselves as untouchable. However, concerned Nigerians continue to demand a lasting solution to the problem. Professor Oluyemisi Obilade, founder of Women Against Rape, Sexual Harassment and Exploitation (WARSHE), contends that male lecturers "see young girls as fringe benefits… We've had cases where the girls have complained and the heads of their department have called them and said, 'Give him what he wants.'"[8]

THE BARUWA SAGA

The case involving Dr. Afeez Baruwa at the University of Lagos (UNILAG) may not have started as a sex for grades scandal, but the moment it came into the public eye, female students felt emboldened to share their stories of how the disgraced lecturer demanded sex as a pre-condition for carrying out his duties.

It all started on 3 August 2015, when the part-time lecturer with the Accounting Department of UNILAG was arrested by officers of the Surulere Police Division for allegedly raping an admission-seeking 18 year old daughter of his friend. Baruwa told police upon his arrest that the sex was consensual.[9] "I don't expect him (Baruwa) to admit that he raped her. I knew he would say it was consensual, but I suspect that this is not the first time he would do such a thing. Let the law take its course, since we don't know how many other girls are being saved because this case is coming out to the public,"[10] said Esther Ogwu, a social worker who handled the case.

A week after Baruwa was arraigned before an Ikeja Magistrate Court, a 28-year-old former student came out with revelations about how she barely escaped being raped by the accused. She explained that the sexual assault of the 18-year-old girl provided an opportunity for her to come forward with details of what she suffered at the lecturer's hands. According to her, she was finishing her undergraduate project at the Distant Learning Institute in February 2014 when she was reassigned to Baruwa, following the retirement of her supervisor.[11] "I finished my project in December 2013. It was around that time my supervisor, who was a very pleasant woman, retired. I was reassigned to Mr. Akinfolarin Baruwa. I got his number and called him on the phone and he told me to come the following day. He fixed the appointment around 5 p.m. the next day. I went to meet him in an office in the Faculty of Business Administration, which he shared with another lecturer."

At the appointed time, the female student arrived at Baruwa's office where another student from the Lagos State University (LASU) had come to submit her project. This indicated to the accuser that Baruwa was also doing part-time work at LASU. As more and more students continued to arrive, Baruwa reportedly directed her to go out and wait for him. "Later, he started sending me on errands. He would tell me to go and make one photocopy or another or buy things for him. I was patient and did everything he asked. He did all these until around 8 p.m. when he eventually looked at my project. As soon as he opened the pages, he flung it away. 'What kind of rubbish is this?' he asked. He said I would have to start the project from the beginning."

After accusing the student of plagiarism, which he said would necessitate an extra year, Baruwa reeled out other academic infractions, all of which were designed to put the hapless girl at his mercy. What followed was too much for the student to bear, as Baruwa locked the door and insisted on having sex with her. But even though she was rough-handled, the girl said she refused to submit to Baruwa. The next time she was in his office, according to her, he was even more aggressive in demanding sex as a precondition for grading her project. At a point she decided to involve other lecturers who might intervene, but they prevailed on her not to lodge a formal report to the authorities.

On 20 February 2020, Baruwa was jailed for 21 years, but he is far from unique; there are far too many of his ilk on Nigerian campuses. A female undergraduate at the University of Jos shed some light on their devious ways: "We have some amorous hawks on the campuses who call themselves lecturers, especially the young ones who do not have much experience. They call you anytime of the day. They have student agents too who they send to woo girls on their behalf. Their marks are not usually based on what the female students actually score. Their marks do not reflect the students' ability. They either give them higher marks because they yield to their sexual advances or fail them for refusing their offers."[12]

Aisha Ado Abdullahi, a lawyer and director of Kano-based Coalition Against Rape and Violence (CARAV), a coalition of civil society organisations working to address rape and sexual harassment, stressed the need for victims to be protected. "It is always difficult getting victims of sexual harassment on the campuses of tertiary institutions to report such issues, probably because they are afraid of the stigmatization that will follow,"[13] she said.

THE ICPC INTERVENTION

In 2012, the Independent Corrupt Practices Commission (ICPC), in partnership with the National Universities Commission (NUC) conducted a study which identified gratification and inducement, through sex or money to manipulate the award of academic marks/grades, as part of the associated corrupt practices prevalent in tertiary institutions across the country.[14] The report titled, 'University System Study and Review (USSR)', recommended a series of preventive actions by university administrators, with prosecution as the ultimate deterrence.

A key objective of the study, which centred on teaching, learning, admissions, enrolment, registration, appointments and promotions - among others - was to examine existing practices, systems and procedures in universities "and ascertain which of such practices, systems or procedures aid or facilitate fraud or corruption; impede [the] quality of service delivery, or [are] open to manipulation and circumvention for personal gain, and creating situation of deliberate or inadvertent victimization of students and staff."[15]

With numerous scandals and media reports of lecturers harassing female students without any consequence, the then ICPC Chairman, Mr Ekpo Nta, made known his agency's plan to disrupt the activities of those who abuse their powers on campuses. "The ICPC is involved in this matter on the basis of abuse of office by these lecturers. They would not have had access to those female students if they did not occupy sensitive positions in the university system," he said.[16]

Nta had been a university administrator before his ICPC appointment, and so this was familiar terrain to him. He was a Senior Assistant Registrar at the University of Cross River (now University of Uyo) in the mid-eighties. He had also served as Records Officer upon the university's founding in 1983, helping to set up the Examination Records Department. He was in charge of the final collation of all examination results, while providing advice and guidance to the Senate on everything from examination records, production of manuals and new processes to the issuance of transcripts. No doubt, Nta would have witnessed his own fair share of cases of examination malpractices and sexual harassment during that period.

At the ICPC, Nta decided to apply Section 8 of the law, which empowers the Commission to investigate any person who corruptly asks for, or obtains benefit of any kind on account of "any favour or disfavour shown to any person by himself in the discharge of his official duties or in relation to any matter connected with the functions, affairs or business of a government department, corporate body or other organisation or institution in which he is serving as an official."[17]

Nta's tough stance on campus predators was strengthened by Section 19 of the ICPC Act, which further amplifies corruption to mean: "Any public officer who uses his office or position to gratify or confer any corrupt or unfair advantage upon himself." Relying on the judgement of Justice Pats-Achonolu of the Supreme Court of Nigeria in *Yusuf v. Obasanjo*, which defines corrupt practices as "certain perfidious and debauched activities which are really felonious in character being redolent in their depravity and want of ethics,"[18] the reasoning of the ICPC - according to its officials I spoke to - was that demand for sex as a reward for lecturers in performance of their duties could be interpreted as an abuse. In short, as demand for gratification by a public officer.

In recent years, the ICPC has tested the law with two prominent scandals that played out in the public domain and helped expose the scourge of perpetrators on campuses. The first involved the Dean of the Faculty of Law at the University of Calabar, Professor Cyril Ndifon, who allegedly sexually assaulted a 20-year-old 400-level Law student in his office in 2015.[19] The second involved Professor Richard Akindele of the Department of Management and Accounting, Obafemi Awolowo University, Ile-Ife, whose audio recorded conversation demanding for sex with a female postgraduate student went viral and eventually terminated his career.[20] In the former, the demand for justice ended on a controversial note while in the latter, the case ended in a conviction.

What raised the profiles of these scandals and elicited media attention was the involvement of the Police, the State Security Service (SSS), the ICPC, Non-Governmental Organisations (NGOs), parents of the victims and the courts. Technology also played a crucial role; for one, it is doubtful whether the series of events that attended Richard Akindele's downfall would have been trigerred without the audio recording that set social media alight and sparked furious debate.

THE CYRIL NDIFON PALAVER

On 29 August 2015, in a letter titled, 'Report of Sexual Assault and Harassment by Professor Cyril Ndifon on Me' and addressed to the Vice Chancellor of the University of Calabar, Miss Sinemobong Ekong Nkang told of her harrowing experience when she sat for a test on 'Law of Trust', a class taught by Ndifon. The test was to last one hour. However, approximately 40 minutes into the exercise, according to the student, the professor ordered everyone to submit their scripts.[21]

As is often the case in such circumstances, students were making frantic efforts to write more, in the hope of properly concluding their work. Nkang was unlucky. Professor Ndifon walked up to her, took the script, tore it and threw the shreds on her seat as he walked away.[22] For a 400-level student, this was more or less an academic death sentence. The implication was that she would not graduate that year. Immediately, the girl was at the mercy of the professor. As she recalled: "All my classmates who saw what happened exclaimed and sympathised with me."

The events that followed were captured in the story of the humiliated student who explained that when she was heading back to her hostel with friends, they passed through the faculty as Professor Ndifon was driving in. He asked if the already distressed girl still had the shreds of the test script he had torn. Jubilant and hoping that God had granted her a reprieve and touched the heart of her lecturer, the girl quickly produced the torn script which she had kept in her bag. The Dean then instructed her to gather together the pieces of paper, get a new foolscap sheet, and go to his office to recopy it.

Keen to ameliorate a situation capable of extending her academic years on campus, the student quickly went to the office of the professor as directed. Her friends waited downstairs, hoping she would soon finish the task and rejoin them. In light of how the Professor of Law later countered the allegation, it is important we take the story as told by Nkang herself:

"I met his secretary and two other staff and explained to them so they could let me sit in their office and write it. He later came into his secretary's office and told me to go to his private office upstairs so that I could be more comfortable since in his secretary's office, I was keeping it on my laps to write.

"On getting to his office, five minutes into when I started writing, he came in with a glass of alcoholic wine, he told me to kiss him with the wine in his mouth and I refused. He offered me the drink and I resisted it, telling him that I don't like alcoholic drinks. He left me and went downstairs. He came back in another five minutes. This time around, he locked the door and took the

key, telling me he also had some work to do while I'll be recopying the test. He sat on his chair doing his work when suddenly he stood up and walked up to me and asked me again to kiss him. I told him I can't and he pretended to let me be and told me I shouldn't worry that I should continue with what I was writing. Not up to ten minutes after then he walked up to me again, and he tried to force me to drink the alcoholic drink.

"On my refusal, he put the drink inside his mouth and came to forcefully kiss me with the drink in his mouth. As God would have it, I tightly sealed my lips and while he tried to kiss me with the drink in his mouth, it spilled on the floor and the cloth I wore. He dragged me up from the chair and pushed me to a two-seater seat in his office and told me that he wanted to have sex with me. I bluntly told him that I cannot have sex with him.

"He dragged my clothes in a bid to remove them, I screamed amidst struggling but there was no way any one could hear me because his office is at the last floor and his secretary and two other staff were in his official office on the first floor. He removed his cloth and bought out a condom from a shelf in his office, wore it and penetrated (me) forcefully and painfully. We heard a knock on the door, he picked up his clothes and quickly wore them and acted like everything was normal then he proceeded to open the door. He left me there and went downstairs with the person that knocked.

"I seized that opportunity, put myself together and tried to rush up and finish writing the test before he came up again. After about twenty minutes, he came back into the office and I just finished recopying the test and I submitted it to him. About to leave the office, he pulled me back and locked the door. At this point, my friends that have been waiting for me downstairs started calling repeatedly because they were worried why I stayed too long upstairs.

"This time around, he came in with a bottle of Guinness Stout

34

which he started drinking. He once again asked me to drink it and I told him that I don't take alcoholic drink. He told me this time it's by force that I must drink. He tried to force the drink through the bottle into my mouth and I spat it out on the floor of his office. He put the drink again the third time in his mouth and asked me to kiss him with the drink in his mouth and I refused, he dragged me, forcefully, opened my mouth and transferred the drink in his mouth into my mouth. I immediately spat it on the floor of his office again. He got angry and dragged me, telling me to strip off my clothes at the count of three.

"At this point, I was tired and exhausted coupled with the fact that I had not eaten since morning. I got really tired of struggling. When he finished counting three and I still did not strip like he ordered, he dragged me to the chair, locked my knees with his legs and started dragging my trousers forcefully and in the process spoilt the zip of my trouser.

"As exhausted as I was, I started crying and begging him that I was weak and had not eaten since morning. He refused to hear, telling me that I was acting and that I'll make a very good actress, that he has met a lot of my type so many times. I finally succeeded in pushing him off my body and knelt down to beg him since I no longer had the strength to continue struggling. He still persisted and pushed me down again, wore a condom and penetrated.

"When I threatened to faint, he finally told me that I can go and offered to drop me off since I was exhausted. I rejected the offer and told him I was going on my own. He insisted but I strongly refused. At that instance, as I was walking out of his office, staggering and very drowsy, he sent me to help him carry his bag to his car downstairs. That's when one of this staff and himself locked the faculty and they drove off."

Humiliated and dejected, Nkang said she sat by a new building beside the Law Library, crying. A man driving by saw the young lady in her pathetic state and decided to ask what was wrong. It was the concerned passer-by who reportedly persuaded Nkang to take the matter to the police. At the police station, after she wrote her statement, Nkang was referred to the police clinic where she underwent a medical examination. That marked the beginning of a protracted battle for justice that involved her parents, the police, university authorities and the ICPC[23].

Determined to get justice for their daughter, Nkang's parents took the case to the media. Mrs Nkang also corroborated her daughter's allegation in a letter to the management of the University of Calabar. She recounted her daughter's ordeal and maintained that the lecturer forcibly had sex with her daughter after a fierce struggle. Five minutes after getting to his private office, according to Mrs Ekang, the professor locked the door, took away the key and advanced towards her daughter, who struggled but was determinedly subdued and raped.

The moment the complaint became public, both the University Registrar, Mr Moses Abang and the Vice Chancellor, Prof James Epoke, in a statement, described the issue as being of "grave concern to management for such an awful report to be associated with a professor of this University and the Dean of our Law Faculty for that matter." The accused was asked to answer, in writing, the allegations against him. The university authority subsequently established a panel to investigate the lecturer; and on 11 September 2015, Ndifon was suspended.

THE FIGHTBACK

As is perhaps to be expected, Professor Ndifon disputed the allegations levelled against him by Nkang. By March 2016, he had filed a suit at the National Industrial Court sitting in Calabar, challenging his suspension. However, in a judgement delivered on 21 September 2016 by Justice Eunice Agbakoba, the suspension was affirmed. Ndifon then approached the Federal High Court, Calabar, where he joined issues with the ICPC and the accuser as respondents. In addition to asking the court to grant him an *ex-parte* order for the enforcement of his fundamental rights, the lecturer sought an interim injunction restraining the ICPC from "harassing, molesting, arresting, abducting, detaining or further threatening to arrest and detain" him.

The counter-claims to the allegations were marshalled in the supporting affidavit for the motion ex-parte. According to Ndifon, he was invited for questioning on the date the student laid her criminal report against him with the police in Calabar. When he reported at the station, he was arrested, detained and subsequently released on bail. After the police conducted a discreet and thorough investigation into the matter, according to Ndifon, nothing incriminating was found against him. Apparently not satisfied with the police investigation, Nkang's parents petitioned the State Security Service (SSS), Calabar Office; and on that account, he was rearrested, detained and again released on bail.

Still, in Ndifon's account, at about the time officers were concluding their investigation, an NGO, the Nigerian Feminist Forum (NFF), petitioned the Inspector General of Police, requesting him to take over the case from the Cross River Command. The matter was subsequently transferred to the Force Headquarters in Abuja for investigation. The lecturer asserted that he was further subjected to another cycle of arrest, detention and bail. As with previous investigations, he noted that nothing incriminating was found against him.

Ndifon further stated that his main concern in approaching the court was that, while the parties were awaiting the official police report, the ICPC Chairman, Mr Ekpo Nta, speaking at a public function in Abuja on 17 September 2015, reportedly announced that the commission had concluded arrangements to prosecute him (Ndifon) for alleged abuse of office. The lecturer alluded to an alleged claim by the accuser and her parents (when they started petitioning the University of Calabar, the Police and the DSS) that the ICPC chairman, being their relation, had assured them that the commission would deal with him. To Ndifon, therefore, the 'hasty' presumption of guilt and the ICPC decision to prosecute as announced by its chairman while the matter was still pending investigation before various levels of the Police and the DSS, supported the alleged threats by the Nkangs that they would use the ICPC against him.

The professor alleged: "The operatives and men of the ICPC are unabatedly hounding, harassing and threatening to arrest and detain me even upon the same incident, allegations, facts, circumstances and matters which are presently pending investigations at the Force Headquarters, Abuja and the Department of the State Security (DSS), Calabar. I also know as a fact that the respondent's threat to arrest and detain me under the foregoing circumstances is wrongful and unlawful."

NTA COUNTERS NDIFON

The former ICPC Chairman has denied any relationship with Ndifon's accuser. "I am not in any way related to the girl and never knew her until the scandal broke. In fact, the investigation by the ICPC on the alleged abuse of public office was based on a petition sent by the victim's mother," said Nta, currently Chair of the National Salaries, Income and Wages Commission (NSIWC), during our chat at his office in Abuja in December 2019.

According to him, the whole idea of fighting abuse of power

on campuses started following the collaboration between the National Universities Commission and ICPC, which led to the University System Study and Review to address corrupt practices in the university system. "This gave rise to several students, parents and other stakeholders seeking redress from ICPC over abuse of processes, including malicious non-release of results, victimisation and sexual harassment. The petition on Ndifon was just one of such petitions received. Other similar ones came from Ambrose Alli University and the University of Lagos," he said.

Aside the petition to the ICPC by Nkang's mother, there were other interventions on the matter. For instance, the 'Class of 1997' Alumni of the University of Calabar Faculty of Law, in an online petition dated 14 September 2015, demanded for Ndifon to be prosecuted.[24] Claiming, as his former students, to know the professor very well, the alumni members, 31 in number, made several damaging allegations against Ndifon before concluding with what they considered to be the critical issues in the case. Some are as follows:

It is against university regulations for a lecturer to hold a test on a Saturday in a programme that is full time. Assuming that the girl had been guilty of examination malpractice as alleged by Prof Ndifon, tearing up her answer script was not the proper course of action to take, as the university has a clear protocol for dealing with examination malpractice issues;

Assuming that the girl had been guilty of examination malpractice, Prof Ndifon had no authority whatsoever to forgive her as she broke university rules, not his private rules. In asking her to recopy the answers on a fresh sheet, he therefore acted ultra vires as a lecturer; and, in covering up a wrongdoing, he fell foul of university regulations. In fact, he broke extant law. There is no satisfactory explanation for why Prof Ndifon took the girl from his office as a Dean, where there were two or three other people, to his personal office as a lecturer – where there was absolutely nobody. The facts reveal that the girl had been carefully chosen as a target.

The petition was directed to the Cross River State Commissioner of Police and several top government officials, including the Solicitor General of the Federation (since the Attorney General of the Federation had not been appointed at the time) were copied. However, there was a contention about whether the petition was authorised. In a statement released two days after the petition went viral, Mr James Ibor expressed regret over "the embarrassment caused to all the persons wrongly named as signatories in the petition" while promising that "an authorized statement duly signed will be published soon."[25]

BATTLE OF WITS

Ndifon's defence before the University of Calabar authorities, set out in his response to the query from the office of the registrar dated 2 September 2015, is certainly interesting. After a lengthy rendering of his own account as to what transpired in his two offices between him and the student, Ndifon deployed his knowledge of law and logic to argue that it was impossible for a sexually harassed female student to behave in the manner reported in Nkang's police statement. Disputing her petition as spurious, unfounded and maliciously contrived to tarnish his reputation, Ndifon raked over the critical moments captured by his student. He wrote: "According to Ms Sinemobong Ekong Nkang, I locked up the office, dragged her clothes and raped her and her screams [for] help were not heard because my office was on the last floor of the building."

This, the professor claimed, was mere fantasy. Quoting

from the accuser's statement as to how he supposedly went to open the door for someone who had knocked, before coming back to further molest her, Ndifon raised critical posers:

"At this juncture, certain fundamental questions beg for answers. Why will a hapless girl who a while ago screamed for help not seize the golden opportunity of the sudden presence of a third party to ask for help and rescue? Why will a hapless girl who is being raped still find the composure to complete the academic assignment of recopying the test without any fear or trauma whatsoever? Why will a hapless girl who is being raped in an office still find comfort to remain in the same office even after the assailant had left the office for about 20 minutes instead of fleeing from this ugly scene? When her worried friend repeatedly called her phones in my absence when I went downstairs, why did she not inform them of her abduction and assault in my office? As a follow-up, whilst her parents alleged in their attached petition that I seized her phones, the student is stating the contrary that she was in possession of the phone even in my absence. Why this contradiction? Who do we believe?

"Why will the hapless girl who had the opportunity to escape stay back until I returned for another round of un-consented sex with her? Why will the same girl who had been raped repeatedly be so 'nice' to carry my bag from the office to the car at the parking lot, and when she met staff at the Faculty of Law, she never seized the opportunity to report the incident to them? One is curious and will like to ask why would a person that has just been raped and traumatized choose not to report to the university's security post which is five metres from the scene, and the Medical Centre which also is five minutes' drive from the scene? These first responders (security post and medical centre) are closer to the 'victim' than the Airport police station."

THE POLICE EXONERATION

The police exonerated Ndifon in June 2016, after completing its investigation. According to the report signed by Assistant Superintendent of Police Babatunde Lasisi of the 'Force Gender Unit' in Abuja, three findings were made before recommendation, none of which indicted the accused. "The evidence of the complainant, according to the police report, [was] incoherent and partly disjointed; there is no material evidence to corroborate the testimonies of the complainant and build this offence of rape around the suspect sufficiently. Sexual intercourse is deemed complete upon proof of penetration of the penis into the vagina," Lasisi wrote.

The report added that the police officers who took Nkang's statement after the alleged incident, observed that she looked "too calm" to have undergone such harassment. *"The voluntary statement of the medical officer revealed that the complainant's clothing was intact, no sign of rumpling nor torn pant, and she was calm as she gave her stories." The report further noted that, upon examination: "There was no bleeding part of her body, no laceration, abrasions nor bruises on her body. On vaginal examination, her panties were not stained, normal female external genitals observed, no abrasion, bruises, no laceration. There was no hyperemia to show forceful penetration within her vulva and pineal region including her anus."*

The Nkangs dismissed the police report as dubious. The ICPC, meanwhile, continued their investigations. "The police went to the scene six days after the report was lodged, at about 8 p.m. the following Thursday, after the incident happened on Saturday, August 29, 2015. This indicates compromise by the police there," Nkang's parents said.[26] In March 2017, a Federal High Court sitting in Calabar ruled that the commission had the right to investigate Ndifon. In setting aside the police report upon which Ndifon had sought to restrain the ICPC, Justice I.E. Ekwo concluded that other issues had arisen which were within the purview of the ICPC to investigate. The judge added that the offence of sexual gratification was contrary to Sections 8, 9, and 19 of the ICPC Act, which refer to any public officer who receives benefit of any kind in the discharge of his duties or uses his position to confer corrupt advantage upon himself.

However, relying on the police report that exonerated him, the University of Calabar recalled Ndifon in November 2017, along with another suspended lecturer, Mr Joseph Odok. Upon his reinstatement, Ndifon held a church thanksgiving service where a clergyman and lecturer with the Catholic Institute of West Africa (CIWA), Rev. Fr. Francis Adeyemi asked him to "forgive" the accuser and her family. "Seek not for vengeance, put your trust first in God, for vengeance belongs to God who is in heaven. For many who would have similar experience would want to seek fetish means for solution," said the priest.[27]

Reputed as the first Professor of Law from Cross River, Ndifon is by no means a small man in the South-South state. This was reflected in the number of prominent personalities in attendance at the church service. "What happened was that they aimed to destroy my career, reputation, the reputation of my family, my village, state and everything that I stand for. They took me and my family through the valley of the shadow of death but God delivered me and did not allow their scheme to succeed," Ndifon told the congregation. *"You won't understand that there was an unseen hand manipulating and directing the movie but in all things I give God thanks, I always saw the hand of God. The fact that I am alive today is a miracle. If not for God, there were many avenues to have brought me down. When the medical report came out, I was exonerated, when the police report came out, I was exonerated and they passed the file from Federal*

Attorney General to the State Attorney General but in all these, they gave the verdict that I had no case to answer; and to sum it up, it shows the favour of God."

Although the case appears to have gone cold - the Court of Appeal did not sit on 25 September 2019 when the matter was to come up for hearing again - the accuser, Sinemobong Ekong Nkang, seems to have moved on. She completed her Law degree with a Second Class Upper, and also made Second Class at the Nigerian Law School.

THE AKINDELE AFFAIR

Sexual harassment has long been rampant in Nigeria's public tertiary institutions, but Professor Richard Akindele met his match in a female student who eventually drowned him in the pool of his own lust. What ended Akindele's career, and ultimately sent him to prison, was a recorded telephone conversation in which he was heard negotiating the number of sexual encounters he would require from the student before he would credit her with the grade she earned.[28]

In the audio recording, Akindele insisted on sexual gratification from Monica Osagie, an MBA student, as the precondition to upgrading her score from 33 to a pass mark in the MBA 632 examination. The clip immediately drew the ire of the general public, which demanded an immediate investigation by the university authority in order to establish the audio's authenticity.

The conversation had been initiated by Monica in a deliberate attempt to use the audio clip as evidence of the professor's sexual harassment of her. At the end of the conversation, when the student seemed satisfied that she had gathered enough evidence to nail Akindele, she queried the rationale behind his demand that she have sex with him five times, saying she would prefer to fail the course than subject herself to such a debasing experience.

The conversation went thus:

Monica: Hello sir.

Akindele: Yes?

Monica: Mmmm… which one is yes again?

Akindele: Yes, editor.

Monica: Yesterday, you said something but because I was close to my boyfriend, I could not say anything. You said you've submitted it.

Akindele: I don't know why you keep asking me. What's your own business about whether I have submitted it?

Monica: Why won't I ask?

Akindele: I gave you an opportunity and you missed it. Forget about it. You will do it next year.

Monica: I didn't miss any opportunity, Prof…

Akindele: I gave it to you and you missed it. Let's forget about it. So, I would just… no, no.

Monica: I wanted to be sure, it's not that I said No.

Akindele: If you are not sure, then forget about it. You will do it next year.

Monica: Is that how you want to talk?

Akindele: Me that I agreed to do something, I know what I meant. So, if you don't trust me, then forget it.

Monica: I am not saying I don't trust you but I need assurance.

Akindele: Continue looking for assurance. If I don't want to do it, why should I give you audience in the first place? If I am not interested in doing it, I won't give you audience in the first instance. The other person has come and I told her straight away because there is nothing I can do to bail that person out and her own mark is even more than your own. The person scored 39 while your own is 33.

Monica: Hmmm.

Akindele: And only two people failed the exam. So, what else do you want me to do?

Monica: Only two? It was three. Now, you have reduced it to two people that failed the exam...

Akindele: I don't know, but I am sure. I thought it was two. It's only two people that have come to me, you can see it anytime you come...

Monica: Hmmm.

Akindele: We are at Moro doing exam. We are doing MBA executive exam.

Monica: They are just writing their own exam?

Akindele: They are just starting today.

Monica: When will you be in the office today?

Akindele: That will be after the exam at 4.30. I will finish by 4:30 p.m. and maybe by 5 p.m., I should be in the office.

Monica: Should I come by 5pm?

Akindele: If you will not come and be asking me stupid questions again. If you are ready...

Monica: It's not stupid questions...

Akindele: But why did you tell me you were doing your period the other time?

Monica: I was really doing my period, Professor Akindele. I swear to God...

Akindele: Stop mentioning my name; and what about now?

Monica: I am not doing my period again.

Akindele: It has finished? And your boyfriend has done it yesterday?

Monica: Is it every time that someone will be doing it with the boyfriend?

Akindele: [Laughing.]

Monica: Is it every time you do it with your wife?

Akindele: Yes.

Monica: It's a lie, not possible.

Akindele: It's not possible. I am just joking.

Monica: So, what's the 411 now?

Akindele: What's the what?

Monica: Plan. What's the plan now?

Akindele: Okay. The plan. Let's have the first one today and then we will do another one tomorrow.

Monica: *'Ehn, se kini yen je bi ounje ni?'* (Is that thing like food now, or what?)

Akindele: Our agreement was five (times).

Monica: Because of… Is it B you want to give me or A? Why would it be five times that you will nack (have sex with) me?

Akindele: No, I cannot, it's not possible.

Monica: Why will it be five times that you will nack me before I go?

Akindele: That's what I will do.

Monica: Prof, you know what? Let me fail it. I can't do it five times; for what nah? No worry. Thank you, sir.

Akindele: You are welcome.

OAU RESPONDS

Apparently embarrassed by the disrepute brought on the university by the controversy, a number of professors and senior lecturers met, a week after the scandal broke, under the aegis of the Congress of University Academics. They challenged the university authorities to launch a full scale investigation into the audio clip. Backed by allies in the National Association of Nigerian Students (NANS), the lecturers demanded action. "If it is established that this is true, the person who perpetrated that does not belong to the academic environment. We are supposed to mould the lives of the students – males and females,"[29] said the group chairman, Dr Niyi Sumonu.

Toeing the same line, the Deputy Coordinator of NANS, South West Chapter, Saheed Afolabi, lamented the increasing spate of sexual harassment by lecturers, while cautioning OAU authorities not to handle the matter with levity. "This is becoming too rampant these days and I want the management of the OAU to investigate this. Although we are still making efforts to know the female student, this should not be swept under the carpet,"[30] Afolabi said.

Faced with persistent clamour for an investigation of the audio clip, the university responded. "We have listened to the audio and we cannot conclude on it now because this is the age of ICT; anything can happen. The university has a way of dealing with such,"[31] said Public Relations Officer (PRO), Mr Abiodun Olanrewaju, who announced the decision to "set up a committee to determine the veracity or otherwise of the conversation so as to establish authenticity of the characters involved. If those involved happen to be our lecturer and student as it is portrayed, the university has a machinery of dealing with such."

Five days after the audio clip went viral, the university constituted a four-person panel to look into the scandal. Tagged, 'Investigative Panel on Alleged Harassment of a Female Student Detailed in Audio Recording,' the panel was presented with a copy of the audio recording of the conversation by the office of the Vice-Chancellor, Professor Eyitope Ogunbodede. The panel was chaired by Professor S.B. Odunsi, Dean of the Faculty of Law, and had the following members: Professor O.M.A. Daramola of the Department of Music; Professor B.A. Adegbehingbe of the Faculty of Clinical Sciences and Mr A. O. Adeniyi, Principal Assistant Registrar (Secretary).

With one week to submit its report, the panel was to, amongst other terms of reference, confirm the authenticity or otherwise of the audio recording; confirm the identities of the individuals involved in the conversation; establish whether or not there was a breach of university regulations or code of conduct; and establish the liability of any other member(s) of the university community in the scandal.

The committee commenced sitting on 11 April 2018, and began calling witnesses two days later. First to testify was the acting Chief Security Officer of OAU, Mr B. Oyatokun, who revealed that the video clip had been in possession of the university authorities at least a month before it was leaked and subsequently went viral. They had prevaricated on acting on it, until the matter was practically taken out of their hands. Meanwhile, as at the time of the commencement of the panel's sitting, the identities of the two persons in the clip had not been officially confirmed beyond social media reportage. But the panel's assignment was made easier by Oyatokun's testimony, which bordered on several independent investigations that he had personally conducted on a copy of the audio that had earlier been sent to him. The Chief Security Officer's testimony was further corroborated by the submission of Prof (Mrs) O.O. Akinlo, a colleague of Akindele's in the Department of Management and Accounting. She confirmed that while Akindele was a lecturer in the department, Monica was an MBA regular student.

A significant detail came to light in the course of the panel sessions: Monica did not fail the course with a score of 33 as claimed by Akindele in the audio clip. She actually scored 45 as reflected in the marking of her answer sheet already submitted by the lecturer and retrieved by the panel. Upon examination of Monica's answer sheet, the panel discovered that there was no alteration. Another witness called by the panel was Prof K. Osotimehin, Head of the Department of Management and Accounting, who marvelled that Akindele could fabricate the failure of a student, purely in a quest to satisfy his inappropriate sexual proclivities.

AKINDELE VERSUS OSAGIE

After a preliminary investigation which affirmed that Akindele was the male culprit in the audio clip, he was summoned to appear before the panel on 16 April 2018. Prior to his appearance, he had exchanged correspondence with the school Registrar, describing the audio recording as "a set up" - which he claimed was orchestrated at about the time he had expressed interest in vying for the office of the Dean of the Faculty of Administration. But it was evident that the lecturer was fighting a losing battle, given the overwhelming evidence against him. "The panel subjected Professor Akindele's narratives to proper scrutiny and found it difficult to accept some of his explanations in the light of prevailing facts and basic logic," the university's report stated. Consequently, OAU suspended Akindele indefinitely while the investigation continued.

On 24 April, 2018, it was the turn of the second character at the centre of the controversy to appear before the panel. According to the panel's report, Monica admitted that the audio recording was her initiative and that she did it without the assistance or collaboration of anyone. The student reportedly stated that she was compelled to carry out the audio recording as proof of Akindele's sexual harassment. She denied being the one who released the audio clip on social media, and disclosed that it was only Dr Folashade Hunsu of the Department of English that she made the clip available to. Monica added that the clip had in fact been deleted from her phone, and told the panel that the release and circulation of the audio clip had come to her as a surprise. Sure enough, it would become clear that Monica was not the one who released the tape.

In her submission before the panel, Hunsu, the Convener of the Committee on Sexual Harassment and Other Discriminatory Practices of Gender and Policy Studies in the university, corroborated Monica's testimony. Sometime in September 2017, she recalled, Monica came to report alleged sexual harassment by Akindele, and consequently made available the controversial audio clip as proof of her allegation. Hunsu told the panel that she was disturbed by the content of the clip and assured Monica that she would take necessary steps.

In line with that promise, Hunsu said she made copies of the clip available to Dr Mejuni, the Director of the Centre for Policy Studies; and Professor (Mrs) Kehinde Taiwo of the Faculty of Technology and a member of the Committee on Sexual Harassment established by the University. Hunsu also disclosed that Mejuni sent a memo to the Vice-Chancellor through the Deputy Vice-Chancellor (Academic) on the audio clip, while she personally discussed it with the Head of Department of Management and Accounting (Osotimehin).

Hunsu told the panel that efforts to hold further discussions with Monica fell through, as the student did not make herself available; and never got back to Hunsu until the audio clip went viral. A distressed Monica then called to ask if Hunsu was the one responsible for the audio's leak; and expressed fears for her life. The gender scholar told the panel that in view of Monica's agitation over the leak, the student could not have been the one that released it. While denying involvement in the leak, Hunsu observed that if management had acted promptly on the memo she sent with the clip, the university could have been spared the international embarrassment of the audio going public.

AKINDELE RECALLED

After Monica Osagie had given her own account, the panel summoned Akindele a second time for cross-examination. He reportedly claimed that he told two lecturers, Prof (Mrs) Ologunde and Dr Neye Olasanmi, that prior to the audio recording, Monica had been harassing him sexually. Both lecturers, who were also invited by the panel to confirm Akindele's claim, dismissed him as a liar. While Olasanmi maintained that the embattled lecturer never at any time discussed such an issue with her before or after the audio recording, Ologunde noted that he only raised the issue with her after the clip was already in circulation.

In his defence before the panel, Akindele claimed that, contrary to the common belief that he was the one harassing his student, the reverse was actually the case. To buttress his point, he tendered the screenshots of a WhatsApp conversation he claimed to have had with Monica on the morning of Sunday, 25 February 2018, during which – according to him – she sent two photos of her private parts. This defence was found to be weak in the face of overwhelming evidence the panel had gathered.

Because the screenshot on Akindele's phone which he tendered as exhibit against Monica was sent from her phone number, the student also had some explaining to do in front of the panel. She denied being the one chatting with Akindele on WhatsApp that morning, claiming that it was her friend whose name she gave as Oghale. Monica conceded that it was done with her collaboration and from her own phone as a way of 'catching fun' at the expense of the professor who Oghale derided as *'agba 'ya'* (a Yoruba term, meaning an elderly person without any sense of honour).

In his written defence, Akindele stated that Monica sent messages to him regularly, describing how good she was in bed and how badly she needed to sleep with him to get an 'A' in his course. He detailed an incident in which Monica came to his office and was caressing his leg. When he shouted at her, she reportedly stood up and lifted up her gown to reveal that she was not wearing any underwear and had a tattoo on her private parts. Monica denied his account, pointing out that she was not wearing a gown on the day in question as alleged by Akindele, but was rather wearing what she described as a jumpsuit. But the professor was unrelenting. "I have a naked picture she sent to my WhatsApp contact, pressing that she wanted to have sexual intercourse with me. I have known this lady to be badly behaved as if she is a psychotic person," he asserted.

The panel was accommodating of Akindele who, apparently in a desperate bid to prove himself the victim of sexual harassment, made available his previous communications with Monica. The record of a WhatsApp chat between the two at 5 a.m. on Sunday, 25 February 2018 was as revealing as it was graphic. Monica's claim that it was someone else using her phone also sounded hollow, but it still did not prove Akindele's counter-claim of being the victim of sexual harassment.

The WhatsApp conversation went along these lines:

Monica: So, you are awake at this time, this will be a good time to give you a blowjob.

Akindele: Yes. Meaning?

Monica: Suck your…

Akindele: Haa

Monica: Stop saying haa. So, when you are with a woman,

you just climb on her and finish?

Akindele: Huuuu.

Monica: Just saying. May be we can try the 69 position one day.

Akindele: Meaning?

Monica: This one is your assignment, Google and find out what it means.

Akindele then sent her two photographs with inscriptions that wished her a happy Sunday to which she sent an immediate response.

Monica: Are you kidding me? I thought you were going to send me pictures of a man sucking a girl's… while she sucks the man's…

Akindele: OK.

Monica: No, it is not okay, let me send you mine but you won't show anybody ooo.

Akindele: OK.

Monica: Promise?

Akindele: Yes.

It was at this stage that Monica sent Akindele the explicit picture she would later claim to be that of her friend. Interestingly, the professor had his doubts and raised a question that suggested familiarity. He asked why her tattoo was not reflected in the photograph. The conversation continued.

Monica: You still remember my tattoo. That's cool.

Akindele: You showed it to me, now you forget that day. I remember everything. But now I want to… you. Since they have accused me of… you when I didn't, why don't I just do it once and for all.

Monica: Yes. I am in Lagos now. When I come over to Ife anytime, we'll…

Akindele: Okay, bye till then.

PANEL RECOMMENDATIONS

In the end, the panel found Akindele guilty of various breaches of Obafemi Awolowo University's Code of Conduct. The panel confirmed that the audio recording was authentic "in the light of oral and documentary evidence adduced so far and which is yet to be challenged or disputed. Furthermore, up to the time of issuing this report, the panel has not got any evidence or information whereby anyone has disputed the authenticity of the audio recording."

According to the panel, both Akindele and Osagie admitted before them that they were the people whose conversation was captured on the audio. The panel therefore concluded that there were prima facie breaches of provisions of the institution's code of conduct by Akindele. For instance, on page one of the code, it is specifically stated: "An academic staff shall not relate to his students in a way that could compromise or be seen to have compromised his position as a teacher, examiner and guardian."

Since the telephone conversation in the audio recording was about discussions, negotiations or haggling for sexual favours in return for examination marks between Akindele and his student, the panel said it amounted to a breach of the university's code of ethics for lecturers. "This would strongly appear to have, or be seen to have compromised Professor Akindele's position as teacher, examiner and guardian. Generally, comments in diverse media that have trailed the audio recording tend to support the view that the telephone conversation was unbecoming and undignifying to the status of Professor Akindele as a teacher, examiner and guardian in the university. (Ironically, Professor Akindele tends to lend more credence to this charge by his presenting evidence of engaging in lewd WhatsApp chats and sending and receiving of pornographic materials between him and Miss Osagie in person or proxy)", the panel noted.

Another section of the code states: "A University staff shall not attempt to obtain from any persons, for himself or for any other person, any... consideration as an inducement or reward for doing or forbearing to do any act in relation to university affairs or business or for showing or forbearing to show favour or disfavour in matters relation to the university." Based on the telephone discussion, according to the panel, the demand for 'five times of sex' by Akindele, being 'a University staff' was a prima facie breach of this Code.

Perhaps the code that finally nailed the lecturer was this: "[G]eneral misbehaviour to the prejudice of the good name or reputation of the University... and misconduct... which has the effect of embarrassing or tarnishing or bringing into ridicule the good name of the University..." The panel took the view that the negative publicity in the social and other media tarnished the image of the University and was clearly a breach of this particular section of the code by Akindele.

On Osagie, the panel noted that her central motive in embarking on the conversation captured on the audio recording was to gather incontrovertible evidence to establish that sexual advances were being made to her by Akindele; not an unwholesome intent of negotiating or trading sex for marks with a lecturer. "Moreover, the audio recording took place after she had learned that she did not fail the course, MBA 632, in question - a fact established by the panel. In this context, it is doubtful if a liability for breach of this code can be sustained against her."

Part of the code reads: "A student shall not molest, intimidate or harass any University staff". This was tested against Monica by the panel in light of Akindele's claim, and she was found not guilty.

SENATE JOINS THE FRAY

Between 2 May 2018 when the investigative panel concluded its assignment and 29 May 2018, there was no information on the outcome of the probe. Apparently fearing that the university might compromise transparency in an attempt to protect a lecturer, Senator Abiodun Olujimi moved a motion calling on the Senate to mandate its Joint Committee on Tertiary Institutions and TETFUND, and Judiciary, Human Rights and Legal Matters to wade into the matter.

Titled, 'The Growing Trend of Sexual Harassment in the Higher Institutions of Learning: The Case of Monica Osagie,' Olujimi urged the Senate "to carry out a full-scale investigation of the case of Monica Osagie and the OAU lecturer in order to ensure that there is transparency and accountability, and that satisfactory justice is done to the victim involved and our laws are further strengthened for effectiveness."[32]

Olujimi highlighted "the growing menace and culture of sexual harassment in our institutions of higher learning; and the psychological, physiological and emotional damage that perverts in our places of learning are bringing upon our children in school as a result." She described Monica as a brave student who succeeded in exposing a perpetrator through her audio recording. According to Olujimi, the intervention of the Senate had become imperative, to ensure that the matter was not covered up or abandoned.

Also lending his voice to the motion, Senator Olugbenga Ashafa decried the tendency for sexual harassment allegations to go unnoticed. "We cannot pretend that sexual harassment does not exist in our higher institutions. This is an age-long behaviour on the part of lecturers particularly. There have been several reported cases of sexual harassment which have been swept under the carpet," Ashafa said.

In adopting Olujimi's prayers, the Senate further mandated the joint committee to "invite the OAU authorities to explain the steps they have taken and the outcome of their internal investigation on the matter as well as institutional reviews they have carried out, together with such further proposals aimed at nipping the problem in the bud."

AKINDELE FIRED!

Within days of the Senate resolution, the authorities of Obafemi Awolowo University, Ile-Ife announced that following the final report and recommendations of the panel which found Akindele guilty of gross misconduct, his indefinite suspension had been elevated to a summary dismissal with effect from 20 June 2018. The Vice-Chancellor, Professor Eyitope Ogunbodede, said the decision was taken after the university's Governing Council received the report of the panel and consequently set up a joint committee with the Senate of the university to examine it.[33]

The verdict of the joint committee of the Council on the report as well as OAU's Senate on the report of the committee which found Akindele guilty of an improper relationship with a student, eventually resulted in the institution's final decision to dismiss the former university don. Ogunbodede declared that "the university has taken further steps to ensure total elimination of sexual harassment in the OAU community," and that the big stick wielded against Akindele would serve as a deterrent to others like him.

According to Ogunbodede, dismissing Akindele was only the proper thing to do, having compromised his position as a lecturer, a fact to which he noted the culprit himself admitted, both verbally and in writing. The vice-chancellor lamented that Akindele's behaviour had brought the university into disrepute by portraying its lecturers as irresponsible, concluding that - in view of evidence at the school's disposal - the embattled lecturer was guilty of misconduct and therefore, liable to dismissal.

Ogunbodede summed up: "Professor Akindele had an inappropriate relationship with his student, Miss Osagie. This was established through their conversation in an audio recording; his reply to the query; oral evidence and the printed WhatsApp conversation tendered before the committee. He had acted in a manner that is seen to have compromised his position as a teacher and examiner, in that his conversation with Miss Osagie was about examination scores and inducement of favour for the alteration of examination scores.[34]

"He offered to change Miss Osagie's purported 33 per cent result to a pass mark in consideration for sexual favours; this was established in the audio recording which he admitted... Professor Akindele operated in a position of power and authority over Miss Osagie and as such sexually harassed her. Professor Akindele was liable for all the allegations of misconduct levelled against him... Accordingly, the Senate recommends that Professor Richard Akindele, having been found liable on all allegations against him, should be dismissed from the services of the university."

THE ROAD TO JAIL

Akindele's academic career may have been terminated as a result of the scandal, but it was not the end of his humiliation. Shortly after he was pronounced guilty of professional and moral misconduct by OAU, the ICPC on 19 November 2018 dragged him before a Federal High Court in Osogbo on a four-count charge bordering on corrupt demand for sexual benefits from a female student and age falsification. Presiding over the case was Justice Maureen Onyetenu.[35]

The four-count charge filed against Akindele read thus:

"That on 16th day of September, 2017 or thereabouts, you corruptly asked for sexual benefits for yourself from one Monica Osagie for a favour that would be thereafter shown to her by upgrading her academic record from fail to pass, thereby committing an offence contrary to and punishable under Section 8(1) a and 2 of the Corrupt Practices and Other Related Offences Commission Act 2000.

"That you solicited sexual benefits from the victim on 16th of September, 2017 or thereabouts for a favour to be given to you, the act contrary to and punishable under Section 18 (b) of the ICPC Act.

"That you deliberately concealed evidence, with the intent to remove parts of the conversation between you and the victim, contrary to Section 15 (1) and (2) of the ICPC Act.

"That you falsified your age by saying, under interrogation, that you were born on April 19, 1961, while in your personal file retrieved from OAU, you claimed you were born on April 19, 1959, an act contrary to and punishable under Section 25 of ICPC Acts, 2000."[36]

While Akindele initially pleaded not guilty to the offences, the judge ordered that he should be remanded in prison custody till 27 November 2018 when a definite hearing on the matter was scheduled. The intervening period provided the ICPC ample opportunity to dig further into his academic history. What they found was not pretty. Akindele's phone, which they had confiscated, also yielded strong evidence of his activities, some of which they would not produce in court. But the evidence was strong enough for Akindele to agree to plead guilty when he was confronted by the ICPC investigators.

When hearing eventually resumed on the matter, Akindele changed his initial not-guilty plea to guilty; and through his lawyer, Omotayo Alade-Fawole, asked for a suspended sentence and plea-bargain. Alade-Fawole prayed the court to grant his client's prayers for plea-bargain in view of his ill-health and the unpleasant punishment already meted out to him by the university, which had dismissed him. Having got their man to accept guilt, the ICPC was not averse to letting Akindele go with a light punishment and then use him in a campaign to rid the campuses of our institutions of higher learning of sexual predators.

On 17 December 2018, however, the matter attained its denouement as Akindele's guilty plea and prayers for suspended sentence were duly rejected by Justice Onyetenu. The trial judge viewed the prayers as unmerited in view of the gravity of the offences committed. According to the judge, the defendant's prayers for suspended sentence and plea bargain could only be applicable if it was in the public interest. Instead, she emphasised the necessity of coming down hard on Akindele, to use him "as a scapegoat without letting the issue of sexual harassment in tertiary institutions continue like that."

Justice Onyetenu, who incidentally graduated from the University, argued that public sympathy was not in favour of the defendant, that many university girls and ladies had been converted to sex slaves in the nation's institutions of higher learning. Akindele had no chance of coming out clean. The judge's exact words were instructive: "The menace is getting to secondary and primary schools. I am a pastor and a counsellor. I know the mental torture many of our female students have been subjected to by the likes of the respondent. The adverse effect of such action is huge. Many of his likes have been awarding marks to those students that are ready to warm their beds, thereby releasing half-baked graduates into the society."[37]

Accordingly, Justice Onyetenu sentenced Akindele to 24 months' jail term for asking Monica for sex, and another 24 months' jail term on the charge of soliciting sexual benefit from the student. For deleting parts of the WhatsApp conversation between him and Osagie to conceal evidence, Justice Onyetenu sentenced Akindele to 12 months' jail term and another 12 months' jail term for falsification of age. Aside convicting him of all charges, Justice Onyetenu also denied Akindele the opportunity of serving his terms in Osogbo - where the prison conditions may be better - but in Ilesha, because of what she saw as the magnitude of the offence, "which is prevalent in the country."

With that, Richard Akindele moved from the ivory tower to prison, following Justice Onyetenu's refusal to temper justice with mercy.

1   https://allafrica.com/stories/201509031150.html

2   http://saharareporters.com/2010/07/22/videotranscript-sexual-harassment-victimized-student-fights-back

3   https://onlinenigeria.com/bin/templates/?a=4395&z=12

4   https://www.vanguardngr.com/2016/11/sacked-randy-lecturer-uniosun/

5   Published in 1958 by Chinua Achebe, 'Things Fall Apart' chronicles pre-colonial life in the south-eastern part of Nigeria and the arrival of the Europeans during the late nineteenth century.

6   https://punchng.com/uniosun-lecturer-sex-scandal-video/

7   https://www.vanguardngr.com/2016/11/sex-scandal-sacked-uniosun-lecturer-ojoniyi-seeks-open-probe/

8   https://www.bellanaija.com/2016/06/unilorin-sexual-harassment-my-colleagues-set-me-up-over-my-rise-to-stardom-lecturer/

9   https://www.inquirer.com/philly/news/nation_world/20070408_Nigerian_women_speak_out_on_sex-for-grades_harassment.html

10   http://www.estherchildrightsfoundation.com/our-cases/Why-I-Raped-My-Friend%27s-Teenage-Daughter-Unilag-Lecturer

11   https://www.facebook.com/permalink.php?story_fbid=477162309125173&id=402044739970264

12   https://liveschoolnews.com.ng/how-i-escaped-being-raped-by-unilag-lecturer-says-another-victim/

13   https://guardian.ng/saturday-magazine/mixed-reactions-over-sex-for-marks-scandal-in-higher-institutions/

14   http://www.chidoonumah.com/concern-rises-over-sexual-harassment-on-nigerian-campuses/

15   https://www.vanguardngr.com/2012/07/icpc-beams-searchlight-on-corrupt-practices-in-nigerian-universities/

16   https://www.google.com/search?ei=9jbNXcSYE8PewALrn7m4BA&q=University+system+study+and+review+report+by+NUC+and+ICPC&oq=University+system+study+and+review+report+by+NUC+and+ICPC&gs

17   https://www.universityworldnews.com/post.php?story=20151024091950180

18   https://www.icpc.gov.ng/wp-content/uploads/downloads/2012/09/CORRUPT-PRACTICES-ACT-2010.pdf

19   https://www.wjir.org/download_data/WJIR0604007.pdf

20   http://crossriverwatch.com/2015/09/dean-faculty-of-law-unical-arrested-for-rape/

21   https://punchng.com/breaking-oau-sex-for-marks-lecturer-akindele-sentenced-to-two-years-in-prison/

22   https://www.thetrentonline.com/unical-law-professor cyril-ndifon-suspended-following-rape-allegation-details/

23   https://www.sunnewsonline.com/rape-of-17-year-old-female-law-student/

24   https://www.nairaland.com/2608083/unical-rape-saga-alumni-petitions

25   http://crossriverwatch.com/2015/09/disclaimer-unical-law-class-1997-disown-petition/

26 Read more at: https://www.vanguardngr.com/2016/04/alleged-rape-unical-case-law-professor-police-parents-undergraduate/

27 http://crossriverwatch.com/2015/09/dean-faculty-of-law-unical-arrested-for-rape/

28 https://www.titiloyeblog.com/2017/11/unical-recalls-professor-cyril-ndifon.html

29 https://www.360nobs.com/2018/04/oau-prof-demands-5-rounds-of-sex-to-pass-female-student-audio/

30 https://www.pulse.ng/communities/student/obafemi-awolowo-university-oau-lecturers-want-professor-in-sex-scandal-to-be/4pnl80e

31 https://dailypost.ng/2018/04/11/sex-marks-oau-lecturers-demand-probe-professor/

32 https://punchng.com/oau-lecturers-demand-probe-of-alleged-sex-seeking-professor/

33 https://punchng.com/senate-probes-oaus-sex-for-mark-scandal-demands-lecturers-sanction/

34 https://www.saharareporters.com/2018/06/20/breaking-oau-sacks-akindele-sex-marks-professor

35 https://oauife.edu.ng/news-events/item/41-council-decision-on-the-audio-conversation-between-professor-richard-akindele-and-ms-monica-osagie

36 https://icpc.gov.ng/2018/11/20/sex-for-marks-scandal-icpc-arraigns-professor-akindele/

37 https://punchng.com/breaking-ex-oau-lecturer-akindele-in-sex-for-marks-scandal-remanded-in-prison/

It is a measure of how widespread this abuse of power has become that I was not particularly surprised to read about teachers in some west and central African countries demanding sex in exchange for higher grades

– GRACA MACHEL, Widow of both former Mozambican president Samora Machel and former South African president Nelson Mandela

CHAPTER TWO

SEXUAL PREDATORS ACROSS AFRICAN CAMPUSES

In September 2019, the British Broadcasting Corporation (BBC) aired a 'BBC Africa Eye' documentary in which reporters posing as students captured Nigerian and Ghanaian university lecturers in compromising situations[1]. In his reaction, the president of the local chapter of the University Teachers Association of Ghana (UTAG), Dr Samuel Nkumban, dismissed the story as lacking in substance. "To title [the documentary] as 'Sex for Grades' is something I cannot duly come to terms with. I don't see anything that directly relates to sex and grades,"[2] he said. Prof Kwame Karikari, founder of Media Foundation for West Africa was also critical, saying: "I have a difficulty for anybody to tell me that the journalist creates his or her own scenario and reports it."

Not all lecturers in the country were as dismissive. According to Fred Awaah of the Department of Business Administration, University of Professional Studies, Accra, sex-for-marks "has become a threatening phenomenon in Africa's higher education," such that in many universities across the continent, "academics, staff and management are reported to have been involved in nefarious acts ranging from manipulating and doctoring grades, results and reviews to trading grades for sexual favours, popularly known as 'sexually transmitted grades'."[3]

In arguing that the power relations that enable the existence of such harassment can also serve to silence it, Awaah used data from research conducted in five higher education institutions in Nigeria, which "revealed that many of the cases of sexual harassment go unpunished and the victims are left to deal with the trauma, which stay with many of them for a long period and sometimes relapses into a psychological condition and mental health challenge."[4]

Interestingly, Awaah also argues that part of the blame should go to female students. "As a lecturer, it is not uncommon to find in African classrooms, female students dressed in manners that are provocative. In such instances where students reveal sensitive parts such as breasts, hips, thighs, back and sometimes panties while in class, lecturers without the moral strength to resist such are likely to fall into what would seem to them an invitation to treat." Such tempting instances, he adds, "are causal factors to the new trend of sex-for-marks in Africa's higher education... some female students who are lazy in their studies sometimes motivate the male lecturers into an unethical relationship with a view to 'use what they have to get what they want', which is a common slogan among such female students who will not attend classes, sit for any form of assessment and would desire to pass their examinations."[5]

However, Sheena Mayenga, a Namibia-based freelance journalist, locates the problem in the fact that power can be abused and exploited for self-serving purposes. "This myopic understanding of power is what has lecturers justifying sex-for-marks. On the other hand, young women are taught directly by their culture and indirectly by pop-culture that sex and their superficial sexuality is a tradable commodity and can be used as a means to an end,"[6] said Mayenga, who believes sexual harassment in higher institutions "will only end if young women understand what sexual harassment is and learn not to abuse their sexuality in order to attain a qualification."

In considering why female students in Africa are particularly susceptible to sexual violence, Christine Dranzoa[7] argued that their backgrounds may provide some context for understanding the challenge. "More than 90 per cent of the younger students are from poor families. Unlike higher education institutions, secondary schools and most homes are restrictive and heavily regulated when it comes to relations between the sexes."[8] This form of socialisation makes for "vulnerable, innocent, unexposed and naïve" female undergraduates, according to Dranzoa. Lecherous male lecturers prey on this naivety, while "other contributing factors include financial need, the imperative to get good grades to open doors to a scarce labour market, graduate unemployment and peer pressure."

In a comprehensive 406-page report, 'Global Corruption Report: Education' in 2013', Transparency International also looked into the vexed issue of sex-for-marks. "Corruption in higher education prevents those who would excel on merit from contributing to their nation's growth and development,"[9] says the report. In a chapter titled, 'Corruption as Abuse of Power: Sexual Violence in Educational Institutions'[10], Fiona Leach, Emeritus Professor of Education at the University of Sussex, details the devastating effect on learning, as caused by the exploitation of female students by male teachers. The academic noted that, while the phenomenon is yet to be globally interrogated, several researches have been carried out in parts of Africa identifying some of the underlying causes.

Despite the adoption of policies against sexual harassment in many African universities, strong patriarchal traditions and weak institutional frameworks have combined to render those policies practically ineffectual on the campuses. The result is that harassment of female students by male lecturers has become quite brazen in most cases. "In higher education, it often involves sex in exchange for good grades or leaked exam questions, and sometimes also admission to an institution or to a high-status course. The price of resistance is likely to be failure or exclusion,"[11] Leach wrote.

The depth of the problem is further illustrated by studies conducted in schools in 15 African countries which "confirm not only that sexual exploitation of female students by male teachers is widespread, but also that the latter appear to act with impunity,"[12] as noted by Yojana Sharma who also interrogated the menace. She added that, "The prevalence in higher education appears to be even greater, with many male lecturers dismissively laying the blame on female students for dressing or behaving provocatively." In Dranzoa's words, meanwhile, patriarchy, "often aggravated by sheer misogynistic behaviour, undermines female staff and students systematically, contributing to denying them advancement and ruining their academic careers."[13]

Dianah Ahumuza, a lecturer at the School of Law, Makerere University, Uganda, locates the problem on her campus in the fact that: "Most of the assessment of the University Exams, especially in the Humanities, are discretional and give the examiner a lot of power in setting, examining and grading, with little redress in case one is genuinely aggrieved with the process." And even in cases where a student has successfully appealed, "the same examiner will be asked to reconsider and re-mark the script. This desecration and lack of proper checks create a sustainable trap and can lead and worsen the sex for grades issues."

Based on her interactions with female students who have made complaints of sexual harassment against male lecturers, particularly related to demands of sex for better assessment scores, Ahumuza observed that these students "do not believe in the available redress mechanisms. They don't believe in a committee composed of fellow faculty members and colleagues of the alleged perpetrators being able to hear and dispense justice in favour of a student victim. Many of them seek administrative remedies, such as having another lecturer mark the particular student, having notorious perpetrators administratively not being allocated compulsory subjects, or having them teach later years like fourth year rather than first year students, for example, where students are more naïve."

Unfortunately, according to Ahumuza, "with the victims preferring silence or not appearing before the relevant bodies because they don't trust them, it's hard for them to get any redress. As a result, many continue to suffer in silence. Societal stereotypes and chauvinism that blame victims, male or female, have greatly led to silence and perpetration of the sex for grades phenomenon. If victims are not encouraged to speak out, the evil can't be handled successfully."

In 2010, a survey conducted by Dr Louise Morley sampled the opinions of some 400 respondents including lecturers, students and policy makers. It revealed a prevalence of transactional sex between lecturers and students in universities in both Ghana and Tanzania. Morley, who teaches Higher Education Studies at the University of London Institute of Education and is Director of the Centre for Higher Education Studies (CHES), wrote: "Interview data revealed sexual harassment of women by men as a discursive and actual practice in all four case-study institutions."[14] A number of male lecturers in the universities surveyed "consider it their right to demand sex with female students" in return for grades.

Due to a culture that excuses the male perpetrators of these acts while criminalising women for the choices they make, sexual harassment is being increasingly normalised on the continent. Citing instances from 2014 when mobs in Uganda attacked girls for wearing mini-skirts, Joachim Buwembo, a respected journalist, is not surprised at the prevalence of sex for grades. "A teacher, or even a lecturer at a university, thinks he will augment his benefits by accessing women who he wouldn't have accessed if he weren't in that position," he said.

The table is, however, turning. Feeling emboldened, young women have in recent months been naming and shaming lecturers who allegedly harassed them while they were students. One account on Twitter was most instructive: "A girl in my class told a randy lecturer, 'your daughter is my friend, Sir'; and the man responded, 'go and give my daughter to your father.' That professor was a serial abuser. (He will) sleep with girls and still award 40 marks."[15]

These are the sorts of stories you hear from female students across the continent.

TANZANIA

Samson Mhimbo was an assistant lecturer at the National Institute of Transport (NIT), Dar es Salaam, until his arrest by Tanzania's Prevention and Combatting of Corruption Bureau (PCCB). The PCCB and a female student had arranged a sting operation after she reported the lecturer's threat to deny her good marks, in a scheduled examination, for her refusal to yield to his sexual demands.[16] Mhimbo was caught pants down at Camp David Guest House in Dar es Salaam; he was tried, convicted and got a three-year jail sentence. It would be comforting to report that all lecherous lecturers in the country get their comeuppance, but that is not the case.

In Tanzania, the corruption of academic institutions goes beyond sex for grades to money exchange in the form of bribes for marks. Dr Umesia Shule, a famous female lecturer at the University of Dar es Salaam (UDSM), once posted a tweet that generated a great deal of heat in and outside the university community. In the tweet tagging President John Magufuli, Shule wrote: "Baba @MagufuliJP, you've come to the University of Dar es Salaam to inaugurate an ultra-modern library. Corruption in the form of sexual favours is widespread at the UDSM..."[17]

In the ensuing controversy, the VC responded that such matters should be notified through the university's official channels, challenging the lecturer to substantiate her claims with evidence. Shule, however, countered that she sent out the tweet to the president only after numerous failed attempts to reach the VC. She further cited occasions where she had reported the matter to the VC's aides without any result.

UGANDA

In July 2017, an investigative committee set up by the authorities of Makerere University in Kampala indicted Brian Musaga, assistant lecturer in the College of Business and Management Studies (CoBAMS) of professional misconduct. Of eight female students interviewed by the committee in connection with the case, six implicated Musaga in acts of sexual harassment. His mode of operation, they revealed, was to work late into the nights and on weekends. During these periods, he would invite female students to his office to offer them sex in exchange for good grades.

Security guards at the institution confirmed Musaga's odd hour operations, while written testimonies submitted by students consistently pointed to the peculiar manner in which he carried out his violations. "The committee noted several similarities in the testimonies regarding the *modus operandi* used by Musaga to sexually harass students. According to the report: "The committee noted that the testimonies from independent students could only be similar if they were pointing to the same thing - the truth. The contrary would hold only if the students had been coached on what to say, but the committee did not get evidence to this effect."[18]

Musaga, who testified before the committee on 19 July 2016 in the presence of his lawyer, reportedly threatened to sue the university for defamation. Undeterred, the committee indicted Musaga of targeting female students caught in examination malpractices or those that failed their papers. Chaired by Dr Betty Ezati, Dean, School of Education, members included Prof Florence Mutonyi D'ujanga, Moses Musinguzi, Goddy Muhumuza and Janet Nabukeera. "Threatening students with dismissal, he (Mosaga) was misusing his authority as a lecturer and supervisor to solicit for sex and this is a basic ingredient of sexual harassment,"[19] the committee concluded.

While Musaga may have broken the proverbial '11th Commandment' by getting caught, the fact remains that there are many like him in the country. A popular Ugandan lady confessed in an interview that she engaged in sex for marks while she was at the university, even though she did not reveal who exactly initiated the illicit transaction.

According to her, some lecturers directly ask for sex in return for favours (marks). One lecturer would say, "I will give you an' A 'if you go out with me". But others might say, "I will fail you in class if you don't have sex with me."[20]

Many believe the situation in the country has created a 'fraternity' culture in which male academic staff members view female students as no more than 'fringe benefits'.

ZIMBABWE

Although the issue of sexual exploitation of female students by male lecturers has been recurring in Zimbabwe for years, a Midlands State University (MSU) student representative, Miss Vennah Makoni, pinned the problem on the exclusion of students during policy formulation stages by government. "There is a thing called thigh for a mark and it's real," she said. "You cannot pass unless you give your thigh to get a mark. I think the policy formulation should include students since it is for students. They cannot impose a policy on us which we were not part of."[21]

The United Nations Resident Coordinator in Zimbabwe, Bishow Parajuli, underscored the need to implement stern measures against perpetrators of sexual harassment, charging that universities must act responsibly. "Close to 70 per cent of students are complaining of sexual violence and I think it's important to look into this area and address that concern", he said, adding that: "Universities must take responsibility and they must put in place various mechanisms such as punishment of perpetrators while giving students confidential platforms to report sexual harassment."[22]

According to a baseline study by Female Students Network Trust (FSNT) in 21 tertiary institutions across the country, approximately 94 per cent of some 3,425 students interviewed indicated they had experienced sexual harassment from lecturers and non-teaching staff in return for favours. The study revealed that: "About 339 reported having been forced into unprotected sexual encounters with lecturers, 209 in sexual encounters with non-academic staff members in tertiary institutions and 902 in sexual encounters with male students."[23]

SIERRA LEONE

Predatory sex between students and their teachers is so prevalent in Sierra Leone that it goes beyond tertiary institutions; high school and primary school students are also at risk. So bad was the situation that, in April 2015, the National Secretariat for the Reduction of Teenage Pregnancy in Sierra Leone launched a campaign tagged 'No Sex for Grade', to raise awareness among female students. But the campaign only targeted victims, with perpetrators allowed to go free. "When he asked, I couldn't say no," said Humu Tavawallie, 14, who was sleeping with her teacher, 37. "When the practicals (exams) came, I didn't have the money to pay. My teacher said I didn't have to pay. He said he wanted to love me."[24]

A newspaper report indicates that, in exchange for sex, Humu's teacher let her off paying school fees and gave her a small stipend. "My mother knows," Humu disclosed, "but she doesn't say anything. As long as I take some money home, and continue to go to school, she never asks questions."

Maud Droodleever Fortuyn, Chief Child Protection Officer for UNICEF Sierra Leone, describes how difficult the situation is for women and children, particularly girls: the civil war that ravaged the country left girls with little concept of their own self-worth, and a belief that all they have to offer is their bodies. "Sex is a currency for these girls. But sex is cheap. In Sierra Leone, girls will sell themselves for lunch."[25]

MOROCCO

On 27 April 2017, in a scandal that rocked Abdelmalek Essaâdi University, Tetouan, a professor of Mathematics was accused of awarding excellent grades to students who agreed to sleep with him. A former student exposed the professor in a series of posts on Facebook, following a call by an Arabic Facebook page for victims of sexual violence to publicly shame their abusers.

The Facebook user posted screenshots of conversations that appeared to show that the professor demanded sex from his students, with a threat to comply or be failed. "After graduating from that cursed university, I decided to come out with the truth," the accuser began. "A university professor at Tetouan's Faculty of Science is sexually exploiting female students in his office at the university, and at his apartment in Martil." The surprise "is that many of the students consensually engage in these relations, but that never stopped the professor from blackmailing some of his reluctant students."[26]

In the ensuing furore, Youssef Agzennay, a member of the Moroccan Students National Union and spokesperson of the Student Union at Abdel Malek Saadi University, informed that campus authorities had opened an inquiry into the allegation. "The existence of such practices amidst the university delivers a striking blow to the principle of equal opportunities, the ethics of the faculty, and the reputation of the university. It questions the integrity and credibility of higher education in general and university degrees in particular,"[27] Agzennay declared.

The report of the investigation never came to light. Meanwhile, a 2014 report titled, 'Sexual Harassment in Moroccan Universities: the Open Secret' revealed that many male lecturers blackmail female students into sexual relationships without consequences from the authorities. "In Morocco, for many years, the sexual harassment inflicted upon many students by unscrupulous professors and the demands for sexual intercourse in exchange for good test scores are an open secret that it is time to denounce,"[28] wrote Sanae Elaji in the report.

LIBERIA

In a country where 'Sex 101' is generally considered a 'compulsory course' female university students must pass before they graduate, it is no surprise that many male lecturers demand sexual gratification almost as a right. In 2011, ActionAid conducted a survey in three Liberian universities with the findings that as many as 85 per cent of female students had been forced to engage in transactional sex with their lecturers. According to the survey, the environment is so toxic for female students that: "If a woman reported her lecturer and he was sacked, the teacher would often simply move to another institution."[29]

Like most countries affected by war, the abuse of female students by teachers is not limited to universities in Liberia. A study titled, 'The impact of Transactional Sex with Teachers on Public School Students in Monrovia, Liberia – a Brief Report' details several of these abuses across all academic institutions at various levels, including primary and secondary schools. According to the report, there is a pattern "of transactional sex between female students and male teachers, which often led to contrived and coercive relationships for the students" – and with most teachers "not disciplined for having sex with students."[30]

NAMIBIA

In 2011, The Namibian Deputy Minister of Education, Dr David Namwandi, announced that he would meet the management of the University of Namibia and order them to conduct a thorough probe into the alleged sex-for-marks scandal raging on the campus. One report said that "lecturers would approach female students with dwindling marks and request sexual favours from them, upon which higher marks are accorded, when such favours are granted."[31]

While the Namibian authorities have tended to downplay the issue, in 2017, Shikulo Eben-esser, Vice President of the Student Representative Council (SRC) at the University of Namibia Southern Campus, went public about the plight of sexually harassed students. He accused male lecturers on the campus of deliberately failing students who reject their sexual advances. "It's the struggle of students who have been failed by their lecturers just because (these female students) resisted having an affair with them," said the SRC leader who claimed that his office had been approached by female students who complained that their continuous assessment marks as calculated by them didn't match those of their lecturers. These female students, according to Ebenesser, were awarded low marks to disqualify them from writing exams after their lecturers were denied sexual favours. "It's no use to come back or register for the same course as they (lecturers) are the same people who are lecturing and demanding sex from these students," he said.

MALAWI

In April 2018, after demonstrations demanding the sack of a male lecturer notorious for demanding sex from female students, with threats of failure should they not submit to him, police were called in before the campus of the Mwimba College of Agriculture in Kasungu was closed down. The student union president, Emmanuel Nundwe said the lecturer told girls to open their legs for him or he would fail them. "This has been going on for long and the students today said 'enough is enough'," Nundwe declared. Since nothing ultimately happened to the lecturer in question, and the culture of sexual exploitation continues on campuses in the country, then perhaps we can say that for many university lecturers in Malawi, 'enough is not necessarily enough'.

It is therefore no surprise that the key findings of a study by Dr Ngeyi Ruth Kanyogolo on 'Sexual Harassment in Universities and Workplaces in Malawi', include: lack of local definition of sexual harassment in law and policies in most of the institutions of higher learning; as well as the "prevalence of sexual harassment especially against female students (by lecturers and peers) and staff; high levels of non-reporting."[32] Kanyogolo also expressed concern at the absence of mechanisms through which aggrieved female students can make complaints and get justice.

MOZAMBIQUE

A documentary by Kiki King, 'Teachers Breaking Trust', reveals how teachers in Mozambique deliberately fail female students so as to coerce them into sex. One female student recalls a conversation with her teacher: "He said, 'You had perfectly good grades. I made you fail the school year. It was me who made this happen.'"

King explains that countless other schoolgirls in Mozambique have been pressured into sex by their teachers. "They are pressured for sex by their teachers and they're told if they don't enter into a sexual relationship with their teacher that they are going to fail the year,[33]" she says. "Sex for grades is where students feel that they have to give up sex in exchange for good grades at school."

While making the documentary, King and her team investigated whether the 'sex for grades' cases were isolated incidents or a more widespread phenomenon. "Everywhere we went in Mozambique, we had a lot of documented evidence that this is happening in big cities and rural areas, in middle-class neighbourhoods and incredibly poor areas, and it targets Muslim girls and Christian girls," she says. "It's surprisingly widespread, and the reality is: it's just another form of men being violent towards women."

GHANA

If there is anything that stands out clearly from the famous Morley Study on higher education in Ghana, it is the prevalence of transactional sex between male lecturers and female students. "The most common form of sexual harassment cited was the *quid pro quo* or sex-for-grades exchange in which some male lecturers considered that they had a *droit de seigneur,* or patriarchal entitlement to the sexual favours of their female students."[34] Regrettably, female students rarely report this harassment formally for fear of victimisation and stigmatisation.

The prevalence of transactional sex has created a market atmosphere on Ghanaian campuses. A female student from a private university was quoted to have said: "We do have a lot of females who come to this place with a mind to learn, do well, get their grades and go out. And we have those who have come with the mind that they are doing everything to get what they want... so if you are the type of person who really wants to compromise positions in terms of having sex with lecturers to get grades, you will get it."[35]

By all accounts, some male lecturers see nothing wrong in asking for sex in exchange for grades. They actually "consider it their right to demand sex for grades."[36] On 8 October 2018, three lecturers in the Department of Finance and Accounting, University of Professional Studies Accra (UPSA) were dismissed for allegedly soliciting sex from their female students. The decision was "to serve as a deterrence to other lecturers who might have involved themselves in such acts and those who might be nursing the intention to engage in them," the university stated.[37]

GABON

What has become an epidemic in this central African country is commonly referred to as "sexually transmitted grades"[38]. Due to the fear of reprisal, however, female students won't file complaints, making it easy for perpetrators to continue taking advantage of them. According to Gabonese law, sexual harassment by any person occupying a hierarchical post is punishable. Yet, sexual harassment stories from female students are widespread. At Omar Bongo University, Libreville, lecturers are said to be notorious for issuing threats of failure to coerce female students into offering sexual favour in exchange for good grades.[39]

While male lecturers argue that they are being blackmailed by female students who supposedly make the offer, the latter category insists that the coercion is purely a use of male power to make life difficult for them until they accede to such illicit demand. Gabonese activists are calling for official channels that would make it easier for victims of sexual harassment to come forward.[40]

KENYA

In May 2018, two professors and several lecturers were involved in a sex for marks scandal at Mount Kenya University (MKU), Thika, the country's largest and most popular private university. While top officials battled hard to save the image of the institution by suppressing the scandal, investigations by a Kenyan publication revealed that many female undergraduates complained about some particular lecturers who exploit their position to demand sex in exchange for better marks.[41]

Off campus, many hotels and motels were said to be patronised primarily by lecturers who were often seen in the company of their vulnerable student-victims. In 2016, a social media user, claiming to be a female student at Nairobi University, posted a curse on her Facebook wall with the picture of a lecturer who allegedly promised her an A in his course only to score her an E after sleeping with her. She alleged that the lecturer wanted to 'ejaculate inside her' but she declined, wondering whether E as a mark stood for 'Ejaculation'. Despite the wide publicity generated by the post of the accuser – said to be a student of Mechanical Engineering at the institution - there has been no response from Mount Kenya University or the government.[42]

This malaise is also rampant among teachers and pupils in secondary schools in the country. No fewer than 1,000 teachers were dismissed between 2009 and 2010 for sexually abusing children. Yet, according to a study conducted by

Kenyatta University in 2009, little or no consequences are faced by predatory teachers. Of more than 1,200 schoolgirls in 70 schools across 10 Kenyan districts who were impregnated by their teachers, 45 per cent of the men implicated were either demoted or transferred. Some were negotiated with to marry their pregnant victims.[43] Only 25 per cent were sacked, while 32 per cent walked away without retribution for their sordid acts.

SOUTH AFRICA

'Sextortion' is how South Africans characterise the use of sex as exchange for better grades in student assessments. At the University of Zululand, authorities invited students with allegations against lecturers who harassed them to a whistle blower service inaugurated by the vice chancellor. This followed a report lodged by a female student alleging that a lecturer was sexually harassing her.

In March 2011, three lecturers from the Walter Sisulu University campuses in Mthatha were investigated for allegedly soliciting sex from students for marks. A final-year student said her friend was once given a question paper and a memorandum the night before they wrote final exams. "I saw it with my naked eyes, I could not believe it. I knew she had an affair with the lecturer, but I never thought he would go that far," she said.[44]

Meanwhile, sexual abuse on campus is not restricted to female students. In January 2019, Gugu Ncube staged a naked protest in front of Union Buildings, South Africa's seat of government, to seek the intervention of President Cyril Ramaphosa on sexual harassment she allegedly suffered at the hand of her manager while working at the University of South Africa. Ncube believed the incident caused her to lose her job. The university claimed that the protester had resigned, but she maintained that she was victimised and later fired unceremoniously for refusing to yield to her manager's advances.

ETHIOPIA

In many African countries where the risk of stigma is very high, harassed female students hardly report their ordeals. Ethiopia is a case in point. Few victims ever speak out. The report of a research where the age of respondents ranged from 18 to 26, was quite revealing. "Lifetime sexual violence was found to be 45.4%. However, 36.1% and 24.4% of respondents reported experiencing sexual violence since entering university and in the current academic year respectively," the report made known.[45]

Another study, 'Sexual Violence Against Female University Students in Ethiopia' by Yohannes Mehretie Adinew and Mihiret Abreham Hagos, submits that the prevalence may be linked to the fact that, "though many women are suffering the consequences of sexual violence, only few victims speak out as it is sensitive and prone to stigma. This lack of data made it difficult to get full picture of the problem and design proper interventions."[46]

EGYPT

In July 2019, a lecturer at the Mass Communication department in Cairo University was fired by the disciplinary board for allegedly using his position to sexually exploit one of his female students. In a statement, university authorities explained that he was investigated on sexual harassment allegations lodged in August 2017.[47]

A most interesting case, however, involved a famous professor who was caught on audio blackmailing an unnamed woman to take off her clothes for pictures otherwise he would harm her.[48] In the recording, the professor was heard dictating a letter to the female student to admit she physically offered herself to him and that he refused. A scream described by social media users as 'terrifying' was also heard in the background. In the course of the investigation, many students testified that the professor was notorious for demanding gifts and ransoms from students to pass his courses, also asking them out on dates at his coffee shop.[49]

Due to lack of sufficient evidence, however, the South Giza Prosecution Office decided not to pursue sexual blackmail charges against the professor, adding that the investigation was not able to determine whether he committed the acts because the reports had been filed eight months earlier.[50]

None of the alleged victims showed up to testify against the suspect, who walked away from the scandal unscathed, underscoring the utter helplessness of female students at the hands of predatory lecturers in Egypt.

ZAMBIA

A research with the objective of determining if sexual harassment was a problem at the University of Zambia (UNZA), more than confirmed the abuse to which female students were subjected by male lecturers on the campus. But, as in other nations across the continent, the problem is a national challenge extending well beyond the University of Zambia to afflict other institutions around the country. Sexual harassment was defined by researchers in the country as an "exchange between parties where one is asked to provide sexual favours in return for something else. In academia, sexual harassment is likely to take this form; examples include provision of sexual favours in exchange for grades…"[51]

In October 2019, two female students at Apex Medical University in Lusaka filed a suit against a lecturer, Philistone Nyirenda of the Faculty of Pharmacy. They accused him of promising that he would make them pass examinations but then failed them when they declined his sexual overtures. In a statement of claim filed at the Lusaka High Court principal registry on 1 October 2019, Sandra Mubanga and Carol Saili stated that Nyirenda was a lecturer and head of the Laboratory Department at the university. "The plaintiffs will aver that they refused to accede to the [defendant's] sexual requests which prompted him to threaten and promise that they will fail the exams,"[52] read the statement of claim. Nyirenda, they added, ensured that he was the one invigilating during the examinations and would often accuse the duo of having sexual relationships with other lecturers in exchange for good grades. "The accusations were made in full view of all the students in the exam class," they alleged.

Apparently in response to the case and other similar scandals, Higher Education Minister, Dr Brian Mushimba, said a new enhanced surveillance programme would be introduced in Zambia to deal with what he described as "the growing number of reported cases of sexual harassment in institutions of higher learning against female students by those entrusted with the responsibility of protecting and nurturing them."[53]

BURKINA FASO

In 2015, the World Bank held a regional workshop in

Burkina Faso to discuss how sexual harassment deprives girls in the West African region of the much-needed education, thus impacting negatively on their economic opportunities. With participants from governments, civil society and the private sector, the discussions were frank and candid. In the course of the sessions, a female participant was emphatic that, at universities in Burkina Faso, "some professors ask students for sexual favours in exchange for good grades." She went on to recount the ordeals to which female undergraduates are subjected not only in the country but across the region. With violent jihadists who believe they must control women and girls, other participants at the conference narrated school-related gender-based violence as a daily challenge for female students who are exposed to physical, psychological and mental torture by men who abuse their powers.

TUNISIA

In Tunisia, easily the most liberal of Arab countries on the continent, female students are currently working on an app that would help expose male lecturers who are making life difficult for them on campus. One such predator is an academic advisor that allegedly threatened a female student who refused his demand for sex, despite knowing her parents. "You know your whole future is in my hands," he reportedly told the student. When her parents took the matter up with the authorities, the only action taken, according to an account by journalist Conor McCormick-Cavanagh, was to assign a new advisor for the traumatised girl while the lecturer faced no repercussions for his misdemeanour.

A 2012 Amnesty International report titled, 'My Body, My Right' showed that the true scale of sexual violence in Tunisia is unknown as it is under-reported. As the report noted: "Many survivors do not come forward out of fear of being accused of complicity in the crime and publicly shamed. As a result, many suffer in silence. When the crimes go unreported, the perpetrators are emboldened to repeat abuses and impunity is entrenched. According to women's rights defenders, media reporting of violence against women is often sensationalist and contributes to the stigmatisation of survivors."

CAMEROON

So-called sexually transmitted marks is also a common practice in Cameroon, where lecherous lecturers coerce female students to trade their bodies for high marks. "The main kind of corruption here is the sale of grades by certain teachers. Students whose work is bad get teachers or education officials to improve their grades," stated a report by the Cameroon Tribune.[54] In universities around the country, female students who refuse sexual advances from some professors do so to their academic peril.[55]

The challenge, as reported in a newspaper by Rabiatou Aiyu Napdounke, is that lecturers involved in such relationships justify their conduct and claim that it involves two consenting adults. "Many students agree with this. However, with cultures and practices that blur lines between what is seen as sexually appropriate behaviour still in practice, these expressions come as no surprise," wrote Napdounke. She argued that sexual harassment and exploitation have become normalised in a society whose culture allows men to inappropriately touch or communicate with women, and teaches women to quietly tolerate it. "Sadly, the sex-for-marks syndrome perpetuates the culture of silence and increases cases of sexual harassment in tertiary institutions.

There have been calls for investigations, but for now, an air of denial prevails."[56]

CENTRAL AFRICAN REPUBLIC

Exploitation of female students by teachers is almost standard practice in Central African Republic (CAR) and it is seen at all levels of the educational ladder in the country. "The very people upon whom we rely to teach pupils how to protect themselves against AIDS are often the ones passing on the virus," Adjibad Karimou of the UNICEF office in Bangui once lamented. Francoise Nboma, head of the English department at a CAR high school, gave some insight into the causes of the problem, and the complicity of many actors in the situation. "Girls often come to school without eating and without proper clothing. They see their teacher as someone to help them. Many parents want their daughters to marry teachers, so they encourage their children to have relationships with them, and the staff don't refuse," Nboma explained.[57]

Pervasive in the country is a malaise which "affects children in schools but is perpetuated in near silence: sexual abuse and coercion from teaching staff. 'Sex for grades' – or, as children call it in many places, 'sexually transmitted grades' – refers to teaching professionals asking children to carry out sexual acts in exchange for regular teaching tasks, such as marking an assignment, or for awarding the grades they need to progress."[58]

SWAZILAND

In March 2019, several University lecturers in eSwatini (Swaziland) were held hostage in their offices amid allegations of sexual assault of female students. The demonstration followed reports that a lecturer allegedly raped a 21-year-old student. "Students stormed the offices of the lecturers alleged to have sexually abused students and held them hostage. They proceeded to write messages on the doors to their offices, making it clear that they were tired of lecturers who abused students."[59] But the efforts were feeble as the lecturer was neither sanctioned nor were there any follow-up by the authorities.

DEMOCRATIC REPUBLIC OF CONGO

A book authored by a former Congolese Education Minister and a Professor of Languages at the University of Kinshasa titled '*Lutte Contre la Corruption en Milieu de L'enseignement Supérieur et Universitaire Congolais* – Fight Against Corruption in the Congolese Higher Education and University Environment' identifies coercive sex between male lecturers and their female students as one of the common forms of corruption in the university system in the Democratic Republic of Congo[60].

SENEGAL

The exploitation of female students in Senegal goes beyond the tertiary institutions to the lower cadres, all the way to the primary schools. An October 2018 report titled, 'It's Not Normal: Sexual Exploitation, Harassment and Abuse in Secondary Schools in Senegal,' by Human Rights Watch (HRW), for instance, detailed a series of abuses by unscrupulous Senegalese teachers. The story of a 16-year-old female student who commenced a sexual relationship with her 30-year-old teacher until she became pregnant, is particularly disturbing. "The teacher denied he impregnated the student when her father tried to make him accept the pregnancy. She in turn abandoned her education as the pregnancy progressed. Fanta is one of the dozens of girls who told HRW that they were coerced into having sex with their teachers in secondary schools, according to the report.

The level of abuse to which women and girls are subjected is high in a country where men see members of the opposite sex as fair game. "I am particularly alarmed at the level of violence against women perpetuated by patriarchal attitudes and conservative values,"[61] said Ms Emna Aouij, chairperson of the UN Working Group on the issue of discrimination against women in law and in practice, visiting Senegal in 2015. "All the stakeholders that I met during my visit stressed the alarming number of rapes, incest, sexual harassment and domestic violence. This is a serious and widespread problem that requires urgent action at all levels."

To end the culture of abuse, especially of female students by male teachers, HRW children researcher, Elin Martinez, advocates that the Senegalese government "must encourage girls to speak out, and send an unequivocal message to all education staff that it will not tolerate sexual violence against students."[62]

CAPE VERDE

The penal code in Cape Verde defines sexual harassment as the abuse of authority to coerce or force another person into sex and is punishable by imprisonment or a fine. But all available reports indicate that the law is hardly ever enforced in a country that is renowned for 'sex tourism' and human trafficking. Therefore, female students who are harassed by their male lecturers simply accept their fate and hardly ever report. Perhaps the challenge can be located in the level of deprivation within the society and a permissive culture that does not see much wrong in transactional sex. "Boys and girls, some of whom may be foreign nationals, are exploited in sex trafficking in Santa Maria, Praia, and Mindelo, sometimes through child sex tourism," according to a report on sexual exploitation in Cape Verde.[63]

MAURITIUS

Laura Samoisy, a freelance journalist in Mauritius, believes that sexual harassment of women and girls is so commonplace that it cannot be restricted only to the education sector. "Whenever women report sexual violence or harassment, the trend in Mauritius and many parts of the world is to blame the victim and find excuses for the perpetrator. This creates a vicious cycle of silence that discourages women from reporting cases to the police and ultimately fuels different forms of gender-based violence (GBV),"[64] she wrote, citing statistics that indicate a prevalence of such incidents in the country.

CHAD

Following his conviction in May 2016 by the Extraordinary African Chambers (EAC), a special court set up within the Senegalese judiciary, former President of Chad, Hissene Habre, will spend the rest of his life in the country's Cap Manuel Prison. But if there was anything that came from the trial, it was the way women and girls were treated in Chad by Habre, who not only sanctioned rape and all manner of sexual violence but actively participated in them, given the testimony of many at his trial.[65] In such an environment, it may be asking too much to expect safe spaces for female students in the universities. And there were none.

SUDAN

In February 2018, in an unprecedented move that shocked the Sudan - a country where women are not only repressed but routinely assaulted without consequences - six female students of the University of Khartoum filed formal petitions against a law professor alleging sexual harassment, attempted assault, and threats of academic penalties unless they provided sexual favours. Although the university promised to investigate, as at the time of going to press with this book, there has been no report and the professor is still on the job.

However, to understand why female students who are sexually harassed by male lecturers do not get justice from the system, one may have to read a March 2016 Human Rights Watch report titled, 'Good Girls Don't Protest'. It is understandable that sexually assaulted female students are better off suffering in silence in a society where there is no "protection as well avenues to remedy or assistance, especially for victims of sexual violence who may be reluctant to report their experiences to others for fear of damaging consequences."[66]

MALI

"The law does not prohibit sexual harassment, which routinely occurred, including in schools, without any government efforts to prevent it."[67]

The foregoing, taken from the '2016 Mali Human Rights Report' by the United States embassy in the country, summarises the ordeal of female students in universities in Mali, who lack legal protection or recourse for sexual assault, even by their lecturers. With poor pay for teachers in the primary and secondary schools as well as university lecturers, a common practice in the country is for female students to run domestic errands, including cooking, for these teachers, leaving them vulnerable to sexual attacks, according to a World Bank report.[68]

EQUATORIAL GUINEA

Since "there is no law addressing violence against women and including specific provisions for investigation, prosecution and punishment of the perpetrator and protection and support services for victims"[69], the issue of sexual harassment of students by lecturers is not taken seriously in Equatorial Guinea. Although, like most African countries, there is no readily available data on sex for grades or other transactional sex on the campuses of institutions of higher learning, Convention on the Elimination of all Forms of Discrimination Against Women (CEDAW) annual reports consistently point to its prevalence in Equitorial Guinea.

THE CONCLUSION

Notwithstanding the foregoing catalogue of sexual harassment cases, it would be wrong to assume that all male lecturers in Africa abuse their trust with female students. Those who do are relatively few. That the majority of male lecturers who are professional in their dealings with female students don't get much public attention is due to the fact that good news hardly makes headlines. Besides, we can also argue that these lecturers are only doing their job as they should, so they attract attention only when caught on the wrong side of the law and public decency.

Therefore, it is important to stress that as prevalent as sex for grades may be on the campuses of institutions of higher learning across the continent, the lecturers who engage in such sordid practices constitute a minority. However, it is also clear from the foregoing that sexual harassment is an entrenched culture and a global challenge that reflects the skewed power dynamics between genders. What feeds and nurtures it on the campuses is what has been described as a self-protecting tendency that compels those at the receiving end to suffer in silence, knowing the consequences for speaking up can be severe, from being shamed to being punished.

Concerned about sexual harassment in research universities, the United States National Academies launched a study in 2016. In the report released in August 2018, the National Academies cited the results from a survey of graduate and undergraduate students at the University of Texas, "which revealed that about 20% of female science students, more than a quarter of female engineering students and more than 40% of female medical students reported sexual harassment by faculty or staff."[70] A similar study conducted by Pennsylvania State University "indicated that faculty or staff were responsible for the harassment of a third of female undergraduates and 43% of female graduate students across all disciplines. The figure was 50% for medical students."[71]

On the whole, the emphasis on male lecturers who abuse their trust in the universities on the continent is based on the danger they constitute to the society. As more and more girls are forced to abandon education for being graded on account of whether or not they sleep with some teachers at practically all levels of education, it is important that the issue of sexual harassment be taken more seriously in Africa.

"The situation is alarming," said Kuessan Sewa, a surveyor in Lome, Togo, whose daughter was impregnated by one of her teachers.[72]

While sexual harassment may be rife in many different spaces, it is the future of the victims that is at stake in the education sector. But as we shall see in the next chapter, attempts to deal with the challenge can also be complicated by the disposition of female students themselves.

ENDNOTES

1   https://www.youtube.com/watch?v=we-F0Gi0Lqs

2   https://www.ghanaweb.com/GhanaHomePage/NewsArchive/BBC-s-Sex-for-Grades-documentary-inconclusive-UG-UTAG-president-787226

3   https://www.universityworldnews.com/post.php?story=20180918104541112

4   https://www.ghanaweb.com/GhanaHomePage/NewsArchive/BBC-s-Sex-for-Grades-documentary-inconclusive-UG-UTAG-president-787226

5   https://www.ghanaweb.com/GhanaHomePage/NewsArchive/BBC-s-Sex-for-Grades-documentary-inconclusive-UG-UTAG-president-787226

6   https://www.universityworldnews.com/post.php?story=20131001155326466

7   https://www.universityworldnews.com/post.php?story=20131001155054992

8   https://issuu.com/transparencyinternational/docs/global_corruption_report_-_educatio/113

9 https://www.universityworldnews.com/post.
php?story=20131001155054992

10 https://www.universityworldnews.com/post.
php?story=20180613143253273

11 https://www.researchgate.net/publication/241711946_Sex_
grades_and_power_in_higher_education_in_Ghana_and_Tanzania

12 https://dailynews.co.tz/news/2019-11-265ddcb748c087d

13 https://www.google.com/search?ei=rwPiXafhBIuBhb
IP2603&q=Shule+tweeted +%E2%80%9CBaba+%40Magufuli+JP
%2C+you%E2%80%99ve+come+to+the+University+of+Dar+es+
Salaam+to+inaugurate+an+ultra-modern+library.+Corruption+in+
the+form+of+sexual+favours+is+widespread+at+the+UDSM

14 https://observer.ug/news/headlines/53663-sex-for-marks-six-
students-pin-makerere-university-lecturer

15 https://www.facebook.com/1411955902179134/posts/in-case-
you-missed-it-via-perilofafrica-sex-for-grades-thumps-uganda-
education-i/1879928448715208/

16 https://www.newzimbabwe.com/sex-for-marks-students-want-
inclusion-in-policy-formulation-stages/

17 https://allafrica.com/stories/201905250208.html

18 https://www.thestandard.co.zw/2015/12/20/zimbabwes-colleges-
of-rape-sexual-abuse/

19 https://www.opendemocracy.net/en/schools-and-sex-abuse-in-
sierra-leone/

20 http://standardtimespress.org/?p=248

21 https://www.moroccoworldnews.com/2017/05/215379/
moroccan-professor-caught-paying-for-sex-with-good-grades/

22 https://www.moroccoworldnews.com/2017/05/215379/
moroccan-professor-caught-paying-for-sex-with-good-grades/

23 https://www.moroccoworldnews.com/2014/02/121854/sexual-
harassment-in-moroccan-universities-the-open-secret/

24 https://www.theguardian.com/global-development/2013/
mar/04/liberian-women-battle-sex-grades-universities

25 https://www.tandfonline.com/doi/abs/10.1080/17450128.2017.1300721

26 https://www.monitor.co.ug/News/Insight/688338-1233818-
ijouna/index.html

27 https://www.nyasatimes.com/college-students-protest-against-

sex-for-grades-lecturer/

28 https://www.marieclaire.com.au/mozambique-school-girls-pressured-into-sex-for-grades

29 https://www.tandfonline.com doi/ abs/10.1080/0305764X.2010.549 453? scroll =top&needAccess=true&journalCode=ccje20

30 https://www.tandfonline.com/doi/ abs/10.1080/0305764X.2010.549453?scroll= top&needAccess=true&journalCode=ccje20

31 https://www.tandfonline.com/doi abs/10.1080/0305764X.2010.549453?scroll =top&needAccess=true&journalCode=ccje20

32 http://www.searcwl.ac.zw/downloads/Malawi.pdf

33 Modern Ghana https://www.modernghana.com/ news/888559/3-upsa-lecturers-dismissed-for-soliciting-sex-from-female-st.html

34 http://www.thenewhumanitarian.org/feature/2008/10/10/%E2% 80%98sexually-transmitted-grades%E2%80%99-kill-quality-education

35 Caroline Shauvet, Mail & Guardian, https://mg.co.za/article/2017-10-23-gabon-students-angry-at-sex-for-grades-pressure

36 https://mg.co.za/article/2017-10-23-gabon-students-angry-at-sex-for-grades-pressure

37 https://www.kenyannewsday.com/2018/05/19/mt-kenya-university-in-studious-effort-to-suppress-sordid-sex-for-marks-scandal/

38 https://www.tuko.co.ke/191035-pretty-nairobi-university-student-exposes-lecturer-sleeping-giving-e-exam.html

39 http://www.thenewhumanitarian.org/news/2011/05/30/ sex-abuse-kenyan-schools

40 https://www.sowetanlive.co.za/news/2011-03-02-3-lecturers-probed-over-sex-for-marks/

41 https://www.ncbi.nlm.nih.gov/pmc/articles/PMC5525286/

42 Daily News Egypt, https://ww.dailynewssegypt.com/2019/07/06/ cairo-university-dismisses-professor-for-sexual-harassment-allegations/

43 https://menafn.com/1098731840/Cairo-University-dismisses-professor-for-sexual-harassment-allegations

44 https://menafn.com/1098731840/Cairo-University-dismisses-

professor-for-sexual-harassment-allegations

45 https://menafn.com/1098731840/Cairo-University-dismisses-professor-for-sexual-harassment-allegations

46 https://www.ncbi.nlm.nih.gov/pmc/articles/PMC5525286/

47 https://www.academia.edu/219009/University_Students_Perspective_of_Sexual_Harassment_A_Case_Study_of_the_University_of_Zambia

48 https://www.universityworldnews.com/post.php?story=2017112906150950

49 https://allafrica.com/stories/200706150852.html

50 http://themedianpaper-yde.blogspot.com/2016/06/sexually-transmitted-marks-in-schools.html

51 https://khn.org/morning-breakout/dr00006218/

52 https://zambiareports.com/2019/10/07/apex-lecturer-failed-2-students-sued-sexual-harassment/

53 https://diggers.news/local/2019/10/11/rising-reports-of-sexual-harassment-in-universities-worry-mushimba/

54 https://www.fmreview.org/sites/fmr/files/FMRdownloads/en/education-displacement/braywatkins.pdf

55 https://theworldnews.net/sz-news/swaziland-students-hold-hostage-lecturers-accused-of-rape-and-sexual-assault-report

56 https://www.universityworldnews.com/post.php?story=20151210074623241

57 https://www.hrw.org/report/2018/10/18/its-not-normal/sexual-exploitation-harassment-and-abuse-secondary-schools-senegal

58 https://www.ohchr.org/EN/NewsEvents/Pages/DisplayNews.aspx?NewsID=15857

59 https://www.hrw.org/news/2018/10/18/senegal-teen-girls-sexually-exploited-harassed-schools

60 https://www.universityworldnews.com/post.php?story=20151210074623241

61 https://www.ohchr.org/EN/NewsEvents/Pages/DisplayNews.aspx?NewsID=15857

62 https://www.hrw.org/news/2018/10/18/senegal-teen-girls-sexually-exploited-harassed-schools

63 https://tbinternet.ohchr.org/Treaties/CEDAW/Shared%20Documents/CPV/CEDAW_C_CPV_9_7314_E.pdf

64 https://genderlinks.org.za/programme-web-menu/mauritius-sexual-harassment-is-an-everyday-struggle-2013-11-27/

65 https://www.worldpoliticsreview.com/articles/24537/how-survivors-of-sexual-assault-helped-bring-chad-s-former-dictator-to-justice

66 https://www.hrw.org/sites/default/files/report_pdf/sudan0316web.pdf

67 https://ml.usembassy.gov/9232-2/

68 http://siteresources.worldbank.org/EDUCATION/Resources/Summary_Book_Girls_Education_MayRIHANI.pdf

69 https://www.genderindex.org/wp-content/uploads/files/datasheets/2019/GQ.pdf

70 https://www8.nationalacademies.org/onpinews/newsitem.aspx?RecordID=24994

71 https://www.insidehighered.com/news/2016/04/14/penn-state-survey-finds-most-sexual-assault-victims-tell-friends-not-campus

72 http://www.ipsnews.net/2001/01/rights-togo-ngos-propose-law-against-sexual-harassment/

Physical intimacy with students is not now and never has been acceptable behavior for academicians. It cannot be defended or explained away by evoking fantasies of devoted professors and sophisticated students being denied the right to 'true love.' Where power differentials exist, there can be no 'mutual consent'

– BILLIE WRIGHT DZIECH, Author of 'The Lecherous Professor: Sexual Harassment on Campus'

CHAPTER THREE

THE OTHER SIDE OF
THE COIN

In 2002, popular Nigerian rapper Eedris Abdulkareem released a song that spoke to the rot in the education sector in the country. While few may have paid attention to the lyrics at the time, '*Mr Lecturer*' passed clear commentary on the sex-for-marks phenomenon in its mimicry of the voice of a university professor asking a female student to see him after class: "*You failed my test, you failed exams; if you want to pass, you know what to do.*" In another track, the voice is that of the same female student, this time making the professor an offer he can't refuse: "*I'm gonna rub your back and your potbelly, make you pass my paper.*"

Despite the skewed balance of power between them, the fact remains that some female students do offer their bodies to male lecturers in exchange for grades. In the effort to rid our campuses of the scourge of sex for grades, this aspect of female students as active participants or initiators of sexual activity with lecturers, in the university setting, can also not be discounted. The issue, of course, remains whether lecturers can have sexual relationships with their students without questions of propriety being raised.

Abimbola Adelakun, Assistant Professor of African and

African Diaspora Studies at the University of Texas at Austin, cautions that even if the sex was initiated by female students, we should never overlook the power dynamic between the parties, which still makes it wrong. As she observed: "There are times that people, wanting to appear 'objective' make the argument that women also have responsibility to not give in to their lecturers. That kind of false balance, the insidious idea that both sides have equal responsibility, can easily become a weapon in the hands of lecturers who want to sleep with their students."

Dr Adelakun pointed out that many girls enter universities relatively young and at an impressionable stage of their lives; and the campus presents their first encounter with authority figures outside the confines of their homes. And while it is true that some can develop emotions for their lecturers, it does not mean the moral responsibility to prevent sexual relationships rests with them. "It is not unusual for students to be infatuated with their lecturers. People develop feelings for celebrities, pastors, and other public figures for different reasons. Lecturers are not exempt from emotional tangle because some of them are the closest thing to a celebrity some students have ever come across in their young lives," noted Adelakun, who believes we should not excuse professors who abuse their trust.

Not everybody agrees with this position. In what he described as stories hardly told, Ugandan academic, Brian Mutebi, has detailed cases of how some female students proposition their male lecturers, presenting themselves as ready for "anything they want" in exchange for high marks at examinations. Following extensive research at Makerere University, Mutebi takes the view that sexual advances on campuses "are a case of well-planned crafty workings by female students to hook lecturers for ulterior motives."[1]

As one lecturer reportedly told Mutebi: "Way before the semester begins, female students find out what lecturer will be teaching which course unit. Once they have acquired this information, they weigh their options and make decisions accordingly. They know that they will fail the exams and are therefore planning a way out in advance to escape retakes."[2]

David Serumaga, President of the Buganda Youth Wing, in a letter to the editor published in one newspaper, argued that criticism from civil society, religious leaders, parents and other activists over the sex-for-marks problem at higher institutions in Uganda leave out those he saw as the real culprits. "I do not support sex-for-marks scenarios or any other types of sex that compromise anyone be it a girl or a boy. The main issue here is that the behaviour is real; some students are engaged in sex for material gains, marks and money from their teachers," he wrote.[3] "Stories have been circulating about how girls mostly in universities, high schools and other institutions of learning have been paying a price in form of bedroom meetings over their marks."

Another piece contributed by the somewhat shadowy *'concerned lecturers from different universities in Kenya,'* pinned the blame on bad parenting: "The excuses have always been 'sex-for-marks' or 'the lecturer wanted sexual favours' or something else. Smart ladies have realised that parents are quick to buy these lines... The students have perfected the art of double life: at home, they are the cutest angels, especially to the dads (fee-paying agents) portraying the image of people in total control of their lives. However, on campus, the girls are daredevils."[4]

According to these 'concerned lecturers in Kenya' who failed to append their individual names to the missive, many of the girls would do anything on campus, including offering sex to lecturers to get by. To the parents, they warned: "The innocent girl you drop to the university in a village choir suit will not be the same girl you will attend the graduation if you will be lucky to grace one." In Gabon, meanwhile, some male lecturers at Omar Bongo University admitted to being on the receiving end of sexual advances from students in exchange for good grades. "Somebody offered to sleep with me to raise her average mark," a departmental head who spoke under condition of anonymity reportedly told AFP[5].

It is therefore worth asking: how common is this malaise in our universities? Is it only male lecturers that should take the blame? Do female students harass or seduce lecturers too? These indeed were some of the questions raised by the Head of Department of Mathematics, University of Lagos, Professor J.O. Olaleru, who argued that: "To sanitise the system, the society also needs to look at the other side of the coin and work on female students to be more responsible. If they are not selling themselves to lecturers, they will be on the laps of sugar daddies in the night looking for gifts and money or you'll find them messing up with fellow male students."[6] Olaleru ignored the fact that this is not an equal playing field or arrangement – lecturers are supposed to be professionals, held to higher standards.

The pushback by male lecturers across the continent has led to revelations about the behaviour of some female students who deliberately lure male lecturers into illicit sex in order to get academic favours. In December 2013, Mzuzu University, Malawi, held a session on sex for grades on campus as a contributory factor to the prevalence of Hiv/AIDS. It turned out to be a platform for lecturers to vent their spleen about sexual approaches from students. "There are cases where students come to us to have their results doctored and they offer to do anything in the process, including sexual intercourse. Such kind of scenarios can only be brought to a halt if students are well civic-educated that the only way one can get good results is through hard work,"[7] one lecturer remarked. Again, ignoring the fact that the power equation is on the side of the lecturer so approached by a female student. The lecturer does not have to go along with the student's wishes. On the other hand, a student facing inappropriate pressure from a lecturer may not have the luxury of just refusing and moving on, because her grades may depend on it. It is a question of power.

In Cameroon, many male lecturers also contend that harassment often comes from the female students themselves. Both Lobe Ekambi, a lecturer at the University Institute of Science and Technology in Yaoundé and Dr Omer Nfor of the University of Bamenda attest to this trend which they say debases scholarship. "I have been confronted with the phenomenon of female students trying to seduce their male lecturers. Indeed, more than once I have been approached by these young students for extra-professional relationships," said Beppe Paul Yombo, Assistant Lecturer at the International Relations Institute of Cameroon.

However, this is not peculiar to African Universities. A study of the experiences of more than a dozen professors in universities across Europe and America found that in several instances, sex for grades is instigated by female students themselves. "I had a girl say she'd *do anything* for extra credit. Her intention was clear. I made a joke of it by responding *Anything? Would you kill a guy?*' I think she was embarrassed I didn't go for it. She dropped my class not long after,"[8] said an American professor.

A Swedish History professor confessed to eating his cake and having it. A female student who repeatedly failed his exam entered his office to make an offer he felt he couldn't refuse: "*I will blow you if you pass me on this class.*" Although he admitted feeling initially "paralysed and did not know what to say," the professor yielded to temptation. "She was a beautiful young, viral woman – and very convincing in her voice. That was the best blow-job I ever had in my 36 years old life. That was a one-timer and it never happened again. Oh and yes, I failed her in class," the professor reportedly claimed,[9] failing to acknowledge that he might have exploited the student's precocious naivety.

While the foregoing speaks to the issue of complicity on the part of some students, it does not excuse male lecturers who engage in transactional sex with their students. In her piece, 'Sexual Relations Between Students and Faculty,' which looked at sexual harassment policies in Canadian universities, Shirley Katz noted that sexual relationships between students and faculty are fraught with peril. The central thesis is that, given the power differential between female students and their male lecturers, the former cannot say no to such relationships, "so her consent is actually coerced compliance. A female student may enter willingly into a sexual relationship with a male professor, 'willingly' in the sense that there is no promise of reward or threat of punishment. But her vulnerability and her desire to please make the relationship always exploitative."[10]

In the uproar that greeted the BBC's Sex for Grades documentary which led to the suspension of two male lecturers at the University of Ghana, a female lecturer at the Ghana Institute of Management and Public Administration (GIMPA), Dr Jemima Nunoo, asserted that female students are not in any way at fault even if they beg for sex from their male lecturers. "In the case of sex for grades the student is never at fault. Even if they are willing. Even if they initiate it. Even if they beg for it. Even if they show you all the contours of their body. You see, the onus and responsibility lies with the lecturer,"[11] she said.

For sure, female students need the full assurance that when they come to a place of study, their emotional and intellectual fabric will not be threatened or crushed. But where there are allegations, the accused also deserves fair hearing. It would be tragic indeed if a career built over time came tumbling down as a result of frivolous, mischievous or false accusations.

While it is therefore true that there are male lecturers not worthy of their calling, there are also cases where offers of sex for grades were actually initiated by female students, as well as cases where sexual harassment claims have turned out to be false. Two cases in Nigeria illustrate this dilemma; and their investigation by the authorities - with one eventually ending up in court - have helped to prove conclusively that in this scandal of sex for grades, while male lecturers owe their female students a duty of care, the latter are also not always the angels they are often assumed to be.

THE UNN CASE

In August 2015, a female student in the Department of History and International Studies at the University of Nigeria, Nsukka (UNN), (name withheld) submitted a letter to the Independent Corrupt Practices Commission (ICPC) titled, 'Report of Bullying, Sexual Harassment, Attempted Rape, Threats and Intimidations by (name withheld)', a lecturer in the Department of Political Science at the university. Upon receipt of the letter, the ICPC Chairman immediately instructed the member responsible for the Universities System Study and Review (USSR), Prof Olu Aina, to set up a special team of investigators to handle the petition.

The team travelled to Enugu and then Nsukka to invite all relevant parties for face-to-face interviews at the

ICPC offices in Enugu and Abuja. In the course of their assignment, commission officials applied different modes of investigation; and the meetings and interrogations were effectively monitored and recorded using audio and visual equipment. Voluntary statements were obtained from the accuser and the accused, as well as additional 'persons of interest'. Documents and devices including mobile phone handsets were also retrieved and scrutinised. To broaden the scope of the investigation, the ICPC team handed out questionnaires to the Vice Chancellor, university officials and several students. This gave them a wider understanding of the various aspects of the issue under interrogation.

Key areas of investigation included ascertaining the prevalence of the 'culture of silence' among UNN authorities regarding sexual harassment, as alleged by the female student; assessing the functionality of available grievance-response mechanisms (if any) for female students who may have been victimised on account of refusal to yield to blackmail by lecturers; collecting verifiable proof of allegations of demand for sex and abuse of office made against the lecturer and recommending adequate professional or administrative penalties, including criminal proceedings if necessary.

The petitioner introduced herself to law officers as a 21-year old female undergraduate and reaffirmed her claim that she met the male lecturer while trying to register for a carryover course. After helping to fix that problem, according to her, the lecturer then offered to also assist her with other courses if she so wanted, a gesture she admittedly accepted. This time though, the lecturer gave a precondition: she must sleep with him.

Her declining the request marked a turning point in their relationship, according to the accuser, leading to the lecturer's attempt to rape her in his office. She recounted his attempts to undress her, describing in graphic terms how he tried to unzip her clothes and how she forcefully resisted him, but not without receiving bruises on her lips and other parts of her body. By her own account, the student was so traumatised that she had difficulty finding her way out of his office to the venue of her examination slated between three and six o'clock in the evening of the same day. She further stated that she was badly affected by the attempted rape and was in shock, a condition that prevented her sharing the episode with anyone immediately afterwards. It was not until July 2015, four months after the alleged incident, that she was compelled to inform her father, upon learning that she had failed the course.

According to the female student, when she approached the office of the Vice Chancellor to report the matter, a member of the security staff tried to dissuade her from seeking redress, as doing so would be like "reporting a case of rape to rapists." She further claimed that the authorities at UNN were in possession of numerous reports tendered by other female students which had been ignored. "Everybody pretends that all is well because of the culture of silence," she told investigators.

Her father, who also spoke with the ICPC team, corroborated his daughter's account. According to him, the moment the matter was brought to his attention by his wife, he called the accused lecturer to appeal to him to leave his daughter alone. He also confirmed calling his friends at the university to seek their intervention, with a threat that if the issue was not resolved, he would take it up legally. He claimed that when he finally appeared before the UNN Senate Panel on 19 October 2015, the chairman not only told him to leave the meeting, he (chairman) also made some "inappropriate comments" about his daughter.

For his part, the lecturer admitted that he had been attracted to his female student, but maintained that he only sought to assist her when it became obvious to him that she was not committed to her studies. He denied her allegation of attempted rape, dismissing it as sheer blackmail. And in a counter-allegation, the lecturer accused the female student of running a prostitution ring comprising fellow campus girls who were regularly ferried around to provide sexual services to visiting dignitaries. The accuser, he alleged, was in the habit of globetrotting with numerous male friends and pimps, suggesting that she was someone who would easily offer her body to lecturers in exchange for good grades.

The lecturer further told the ICPC team that there were two main reasons why the student and her father were 'persecuting' him. One, his 'refusal' to accept the bribe he claimed they offered him to influence her results. The second was his subsequent marriage to another woman, insinuating that the girl had hoped that she would be his bride. As the investigation progressed, academic and non-academic staff of the university, including a lecturer and the exams and records officer, made statements.

The ICPC team was gender-sensitive in composition; members included two men and two women. Tendering her first year results at the university and other academic credentials obtained as a student of the Federal Government Academy for Gifted Children, which she said earned her admission into UNN on merit, the student portrayed herself as brilliant, diligent and hardworking - and that she was being sexually harassed, victimised and frustrated by a corrupt educational system. The team indeed noted, based on her demeanour and composure, that the student was bold, confident, calm and articulate even under pressure.

However, according to the ICPC officials I spoke to, her

story did not add up. For instance, contrary to the allegation of a culture of silence' regarding allegations of sexual harassment at the university, the investigation revealed that the Vice Chancellor had acted promptly upon receipt of the complaint she filed on 7 August, 2015, and directed both the Registrar and Security Unit to investigate the allegations immediately. The VC also directed that the lecturer be suspended from duty, with half salary, pending the investigation of the case by a special UNN/Council panel constituted for the purpose.

These facts were corroborated by the statements of the UNN professors who were also friends to the accuser's father. They were also corroborated by the two officers in the security unit assigned to investigate the case. Asked to mention similar incidents that were not investigated because of the purported culture of silence, the complainant could not cite any. Accordingly, the ICPC investigation found no evidence of conspiracy or abetment of abuse of office and demand for sexual gratification against the management of the university on that score. Intent on getting to the root of the matter, the ICPC team dug deeper and found a treasure trove of information as a result of forensic analysis carried out on the mobile handsets owned by the principal characters.

When the student and her lecturer began communicating, sending and receiving SMS and WhatsApp chats, it probably never occurred to them that they could be creating potential evidence for charges and defence. And so, while the student alleged that the lecturer used his position of power to intimidate, threaten and sexually harass her by direct word of mouth, telephone calls and WhatsApp messages, forensic investigation found no evidence to support her claims. The ICPC report validated the conclusion arrived at by UNN that the circumstantial evidence supporting the accusation of rape said to have occurred on 2 March 2015, as presented by the female student, was "fictitious and never existed."

Furthermore, the ICPC team discovered that in an attempt to mislead, the student had deliberately doctored WhatsApp messages between her and the lecturer; and, "she refused to answer any further questions or offer any explanations on the observed discrepancies during the last interview she had with the ICPC team." The findings of the ICPC team at the end of their investigation were at variance with the claims made by the accuser. Contrary to the allegation that the lecturer invited the student to his office before the GSP 201 examination on 2 March 2015 via telephone calls, for instance, "the unabridged WhatsApp chat between them revealed that it was actually the female student who initiated conversation with her lecturer as early as 4:34 a.m. on that day." When the lecturer replied at 9:30 a.m., the student complained about a fire incident in her hostel that left her "shaking" and unable to focus or prepare for the two examinations she was scheduled to take between 12 to 3 p.m. and 3 to 6 p.m. respectively later that day. Her reply contained a suggestive line to the effect that she was so shaken by the fire incident that she "Cud (sic) use some meaningful company right now."

Urging the student to remain calm, the lecturer invited her to his office to study and prepare for the examination by 11:00 a.m., an invitation she accepted. According to the ICPC, the student "never mentioned, admitted or agreed to answer question from the team relating to her being in the office of the first respondent (the lecturer) between 11 to 12 a.m. or at any time prior to 3:30 p.m. on 2 March 2015 when she claimed that the first respondent attempted to rape her." The investigation, the ICPC report stated further, "did not find any evidence to contradict the findings of UNN security investigators that the scheduled test started at 3 p.m. and lasted for 1 hour 30 minutes. This contradicts the petitioner's claim that the examination had ended by the time she found her way from the first respondent's office at 4:05 p.m. to the examination hall at 4:10 p.m."

Below are excerpts from the ICPC report:

(The student) claimed that the lecturer demanded for sexual gratification in order to assist her to pass an examination she did not sit for. But she did not report the incident of alleged rape until four months later after the result of the examination was out and she failed. Meanwhile, ICPC investigation did not find any evidence to establish that the lecturer was in a direct supervisory role or had the necessary clout to directly or indirectly influence the result of an examination (female student) did not sit for.

The team obtained a copy of UNN Undergraduate Academic Regulations and observed among others that (the female student) did not comply with Regulation No.5 (ii) which makes it mandatory for any student prevented from sitting any examination for reasons other than ill health to report to the Registrar through the relevant Head of Department within 48 hours after such examination.

Very significantly, manual examination of the Blackberry Q10 model GSM handset of (female student) further revealed a recorded incidence between the duo on the 12th March, 2015 while in the office of the lecturer. The incidence was jovial, with both parties laughing heartily and parting without recriminations. The timestamp of the audio recording on (female student's) handset gave the exact date of the conversation but she refused to comment on the recording when questioned by the Team.

The more ICPC investigated the case, the more glaring it became that this was not a case of sexual harassment but that of a relationship between the duo that hinted at several other things. Apparently sensing that the investigation was not going her way, the student began to duck, failing to demonstrate the kind of enthusiasm exhibited at the beginning. The report of the UNN panel investigation provided to the ICPC team offers some clues. The student, it was noted, refused to honour an earlier invitation to appear before the UNN panel investigating her case on 28 September 2015. She also insisted that she would not honour the second invitation to attend the UNN Senate/Council panel session on 19 and 20 October 2015 unless the ICPC team accompanied her, disguised as members of her family.

By this time, facts were coming to light on the only mobile phone she initially submitted to the ICPC team, which she was now attempting to retrieve. Investigations confirmed that the student adopted "Mysteria" and "Bentley" as pseudonyms in her various WhatsApp chats. Forensic analysis of her iPhone showed that she had persuaded and coached her father, said to be a humble public officer, to make threatening phone calls to UNN investigators and officers. His testimony before the UNN panel on 20 October 2015 was therefore suspect, hence the shabby treatment meted to him by the university authorities.

As the ICPC team began to review narratives and ask more probing questions, the student became evasive and uncooperative, especially when the truth about her petition had begun to unravel, and with it, the apparent motive. In trying to unearth the truth or otherwise of her charges, the ICPC team stumbled on details of the intimate nature of her relationships with other lecturers.

Here is what the ICPC team had to say about that:

Investigation focused on the personal lifestyle of (female student) and the findings corroborated the allegations that she was doing more on campus than studying. She was in sexual relationships with different men, including her lecturers. A review of unabridged texts of separate WhatsApp chats between her, (female student) and one other individual identified on her phone simply as ABC were sexually explicit and obscene. The lurid chats and photographs also reveal the carnal mindset of the participants. The WhatsApp chats with ABC revealed that the lecturer who claims to be on the Department Examination Committee offered to use his position to alter her academic scores in a number of courses, particularly the course he lectures. Some passages in the chat suggest that the said ABC may in fact have written the final year project for her. In one of the chats, she hinted at a more than casual friendship by stating that they were not only "stupid friends but emotionally attached" to each other.

That there was an inappropriate relationship between the lecturer and the student was not in doubt. But it appeared to be a consensual relationship that was not at any point coerced. Besides, the allegation being investigated was that of attempted rape. And that could not be supported by any evidence. A physical examination of the Gionee GSM handset of (female student) revealed various contents ranging from academic and social discourse to visually explicit photographs and adult video clips...

In the end, the ICPC team agreed with the conclusion of the UNN investigation report that the student might have been using "Machiavellian tactic" against the lecturer in order to eat her cake and still have it. "Unless the petitioner is able to offer reasonable explanation for the apparent alteration of WhatsApp chats, withholding and destruction of evidence on Blackberry Q10 phone, the investigation is unable to come to a different conclusion from the UNN Investigation Report."

What the case revealed quite clearly was that the student was in the habit of initiating transactional sex to 'upgrade' her academic scores. But there was also a curious twist: The lecturer was spotted wearing brassieres and other female undergarments in photographs found on his mobile phones. Not even the explanation that he snapped them while observing a private moment with his wife could rid him of resultant speculation concerning his sexuality.

Parting shots from members of the ICPC team in their interim report were reflective of the nature of their assignment, the characters involved in the conflict, the seriousness that went into the pursuit of justice and their own personal integrity. The team noted that the student tried to influence the inquiry by inviting the leader of the ICPC team for an all-night date on Saturday 24 October 2015. Meanwhile, she made a verbal complaint to a male officer of the commission that the said team leader was sexually harassing her, and sought the officer's assistance to get her phones released. What she did not know was that her interactions with this particular ICPC official were on record, including suggestive photographs she sent to him.

Despite how the UNN case panned out, there are reasons why sexual assault in whatever form cannot be taken lightly. Chief among them are the direct consequences for the abused. Even when there are no apparent physical scars, the emotional and psychological wounds can be devastating. Research has shown that there are established cases of bipolar affective disorders, unwanted pregnancies, suicidal thoughts and actions, insomnia, drug abuse, alcoholism, disassociation, sexually transmitted diseases and other health conditions directly traceable to misdirected sexual activities on campuses. The odd false accusation notwithstanding, it is clear that allegations of sexual abuse must be treated with seriousness by universities and all relevant authorities.

THE CHARGE AGAINST OTUBU

In July 2010, the video of an Engineering lecturer at Ambrose Alli University, Ekpoma, identified as Peter Otubu, sparked immediate social media frenzy when it surfaced on YouTube.[12] The video showed Otubu stripped by female students when he was caught in the room of Judith Okosun, a 400-level student of Electrical and Electronics Engineering the lecturer was allegedly sleeping with in exchange for marks. The students recorded themselves humiliating the lecturer verbally and physically.

Before they released him, the lecturer was made to sign a N100,000 cheque to placate Judith, with the assurance that the video would not be released nor the incident reported to school authorities. He was also warned against involving the police. But the moment he secured his freedom, the lecturer ran straight to the police station and reported that he had been kidnapped by the students. Judith was subsequently arrested and detained for two days at the State Criminal Investigation Department (SCID). By then the video had gone viral.

When the then Edo State Governor Adams Oshiomhole got wind of the incident, he directed the management of the state-owned university to investigate the allegation of sexual harassment against the lecturer.[13] After setting up two committees to investigate the matter, the university terminated Dr Otubu's appointment on 26 October 2010. Six months later in March 2011, Judith was also suspended for six semesters, having been found guilty of "breaching her matriculation oath."[14]

According to the university Vice Chancellor, Professor Sam Uniamikogbo, "The student was aware of the university's rules and regulations and once any student violates any of the rules, that student will be disciplined." The rules forbid students from taking laws into their own hands, as Judith did by detaining and extorting the lecturer. But that was not the end of the matter, as Judith went to court to challenge her rustication from Ambrose Alli University, Ekpoma.

TWIST IN THE TALE

Following investigations, however, it was discovered that the entire episode was orchestrated by Judith in concert with three lecturers and a number of hoodlums. Although the ex parte application by Police to the Federal High Court, sitting in Benin, to compel MTN Nigeria to release full SMS messages and audio version of communications between Judith and her lecturers failed, investigations nonetheless confirmed that Otubu had been involved in a sexual relationship with Judith.

Explaining the motive for the entrapment, Otubu said that in the course of one examination, he noticed that some students smuggled booklets out of the hall and returned to submit detailed answers with the aid of text books. Otubu then devised ways of checkmating the students and also helped to expose a lecturer who was their enabler. Regarding Judith, Otubu had this to say: "This relationship was, in fact, initiated by the said Judith Ivie Okosun by sending an SMS message to my phone, expressing her love feelings to me. We exchanged phone calls and SMS messages but I later discovered that she didn't possess the inherent qualities of a good partner."[15] What he never bargained for was that Judith would bring him down.

According to Otubu, Judith had come to him to say that she did badly in the examination. "She requested me to allow her rewrite the said paper outside the university but I sharply rebuked her and told her it was impossible. This request was made by her on Friday, 16 July 2010, and my ordeal in her hands and the other hoodlums happened on the 17th day of July, 2010," the beleaguered lecturer said.

In August 2012, seven persons were charged before an Ekpoma Magistrates' Court on a seven-count charge of alleged stealing, threat to kill, unlawful detention and publication, false statement and assault punishable under the criminal procedure law. Those charged before the court were: Samson Ogbeide, Igbudu Samuel and Ojeabulu Eghosa Clement, all lecturers of AAU as well as Judith Ivie Okosun, Juliet Obehi Okosun, Esther Ogbeide and Aruya Ohis William.[16]

The accused persons were said to have conspired to commit felony with intent to steal and demand the sum of N500,000 from Dr Peter Otubu with threat to kill or lynch him if he failed to comply, which made him issue a cheque of N100,000 in favour of Judith Ivie Okosun, an offence punishable under sections 516, 406, 390(a) of the criminal code. The accused persons were also alleged to have unlawfully detained Otubu in Judith's apartment against his will, as well as record and publish the video clips of the plaintiff (Otubu) on the internet with intent to injure and expose him to hatred; an offence punishable under sections 365, 573, 375, 126, 125(a), 355 of the criminal codes.

The trial lasted six years but when it eventually concluded in 2018, Chief Magistrate Maltina Iluobe sentenced Juliet Obehi Okosun to two-years imprisonment for unlawful detention and indecent assault on a university don, having established against her the crime of entrapment, "which resulted in the show of shame, humiliation and torture. This court is of the view that there is a very strong conspiracy and set up against Dr Peter Otubu."[17] Judith Ivie Okosun got a one year jail term.

Although the magistrate scolded Otubu for suffering

"from the sins of immorality to have gone to the room of his student which resulted in the show of shame," the lecturer expressed satisfaction that he was exonerated of wrongdoing. He said: "I am okay. The principal suspect, Ivie Okosun and her sister, Juliet Obehi Okosun, have been convicted and jailed, whether they were given an option of fine or not. My appointment was terminated following the video that was posted on the Internet."[18]

Despite being vindicated on the charge of rape, Otubu paid a heavy price for his indiscretion. He had joined the university as a non-academic staff in 1983 and rose to the position of Chief Engineer and converted to an academic staff as Lecturer II in 2010, following the completion of his doctorate degree in Engineering. His more than 32-year career ended with a visit to his female student who set him up for humiliation.

CONCLUSION

At the end, the foregoing cases are perfect examples of what happens when people cross all kinds of boundaries either because they lack personal discipline or they have no ethical awareness. When lecturers let down their moral guards as authority figures, they not only give room for all kinds of disrespect, they also make themselves vulnerable to all manner of mischief. While we will never fully understand the motivation of the female students involved in the aforementioned cases, we can put safeguards in place to deter future occurrence.

ENDNOTES

1   Mutebi, an award-winning journalist and girls' rights campaigner, is the founder of Education Development Opportunity, Uganda (EDOU), described as "one of Africa's leading women rights crusaders" for his extensive writing and advocacy for girls' and women's rights

2   https://www.newvision.co.ug/new_vision/news/1469721/sex-marks-tall-varsities

3   https://eagle.co.ug/2018/03/02/blaming-lecturers-sex-marks-students.html

4   https://citizentv.co.ke/blogs/parents-to-blame-for-university-girls-leading-secret-lives-211473/

5   https://www.france24.com/en/20171022-gabon-students-angry-sex-grades-pressure

6   https://thenationonlineng.net/sex-for-marks-and-the-complicity-of-bbc-africa/

7   https://www.nyasatimes.com/exposed-malawi-students-opt-for-sex-with-lecturers-to-have-grades-doctored/

8   https://didyouknowfacts.com/15-teachers-students-sex-grades/

9   https://didyouknowfacts.com/15-teachers-students-sex-grades/

10   https://www.universityaffairs.ca/opinion/in-my-opinion/sexual-relations-students-faculty/

11   https://theworldnews.net/gh-news/sex-for-grades-students-not-at-fault-even-if-they-beg-for-it-gimpa-lecturer

12   https://www.facebook.com/newsbytesnow/videos/video-of-another-randy-lecturer-mr-okosun-caught-pants-down-with-female-student-/1437586016348174/

13   http://saharareporters.com/2010/07/23/edo-governor-orders-probe-ambrose-alli-varsity's-sex-grade-scandal

14   http://saharareporters.com/2011/03/02/ambrose-alli-university-sex-grades-update-dr-otubu-fired-judith-okosun-suspended-six

15   http://ekpoma-allegedrandylecturer.blogspot.com/

16   https://www.pmnewsnigeria.com/2018/04/22/2-aau-female-graduates-who-accused-lecturer-of-sex-for-grade-jailed/

17   https://allafrica.com/stories/201804230041.html

18   https://www.sunnewsonline.com/show-shame-students-convicted-disgraced-lecturer/

From the first day I walked into class, the lecturer must have noticed I was a new student trying to catch up. One time I told him the students would like more copies of the lecture notes. He told me to go to his office. When I got there, he closed the curtains, closed the door and so many things happened...
There's a lot of guilt. One of my greatest fears is being misunderstood ... I was petrified and didn't want my grades to be affected. I'm a student leader; I worried the other students might not believe me. They know me as a very vocal person, and here I am struggling with my own problems, suffering silently. I felt like I didn't have a choice.

– DIANA, 20-year-old. One of the speakers at the launch of #CampusMeToo, a campaign by ActionAid and UN Women in Nairobi, Kenya

CHAPTER FOUR

CURBING SEXUAL
EXPLOITATION

Following an investigation which revealed that some male lecturers were in the habit of demanding that female students present their homework in person at awkward hours and in private locations, authorities at Makerere University in Uganda have directed that lecturers should always leave their office doors open anytime students are with them. Consultations with students are also mandated to be on university premises, with departmental heads informed ahead of those engagements. The policy further states that what women wear is not a valid defence for sexual harassment. The revisions followed recommendations by the Professor Sylvia Tamale Committee, which concluded that while the onus for lodging a formal complaint on sexual harassment rests with the victim, anonymous complaints should never be ignored. Additionally, the authorities were enjoined to provide full support for counselling and medical care to victims of sexual harassment.

The foregoing is just one of the many ways in which universities across Africa have tried to confront the problem of sexual harassment on campuses. But these measures still do not adequately address the problem in its facets. To be clear, whether on the campus or in the workplace, sexual misconduct is a global challenge that has existed for generations, and it is one that has become so normalised that there were never serious or sustained public discussions about it. That was until 15 October 2017 when American actress Alyssa Milano, motivated by a New York Times report precipitating the downfall of powerful Hollywood film producer, Harvey Weinstein, tweeted: "If you've been sexually harassed or assaulted, write 'me too' as a reply to this tweet."

The tweet by Milano marked the start of a propulsive new phase for the #*MeToo* hashtag, which took off from a movement started by activist Tarana Burke in 2006 to campaign against sexual abuse and assault. The hashtag would go on to be used more than 500,000 times on Twitter within the next 24 hours. Notable among users were: superstar singer, Lady Gaga; actresses Rosario Dawson, Anna Paquin and Evan Rachel Wood; as well as Najwa Zebian, a poet. At the end, what made Weinstein's fall exceptional is the calibre of people who came out to accuse him of sexual misconduct. Stars like Ashley Judd, Angelina Jolie and Gwyneth Paltrow broke the wall of silence about issues that were previously hushed or settled; and facilitated a conversation that exposed a long list of abusers as well as enablers of the sexual abuse of women and girls.

Although the hashtag originated in the United States, the reverberation was global. Women and girls across the world suddenly found their voices as they joined in the conversation - writing, speaking and sharing their experience with the hashtag, #*MeToo*'. In a project titled, 'The #*MeToo* Stories You Haven't Heard', CNN Africa featured women from different background who recounted their experiences of rape, sexual abuse and assault at the hands of men they encountered in their offices, at schools, homes and churches. But the #*MeToo* movement never gained much momentum on the African continent, due largely to a patriarchal culture in which those who dare to speak out about sexual harassment and assault are stigmatised. This has inadvertently encouraged indifference, with victims invariably refusing or unable to speak out. Unfortunately, this only helps the perpetrators to get away.

What perhaps forced the issue into the public consciousness was the September 2019 'BBC Africa Eye documentary' titled, 'Sex for Grades'. Narrating her personal ordeal on camera, Kiki Mordi, who anchored the investigation, said her exam results were withheld for two semesters because she refused the sexual advances of a professor; and when it became clear that she would never get justice from the system, she dropped out of university. "I'm a 28-year-old who never got to finish school because of one thing," said Mordi. "It wasn't because I wasn't brilliant or anything – I was a high flyer when I was growing up. But I didn't even finish. All because of sexual harassment."

She is just one of countless women whose academic dreams have been shattered. Sexual violence in universities across the continent - according to a French Ministry of Foreign Affairs Report authored by Marie Devers, Paule Élise Henry, Élisabeth Hofmann and Halim Benabdallah - arises from "the dimension of social relations between men and women as well as unequal power between genders." The authors identified some of the obstacles to include the "absence of any support service and stigmatisation of victims and survivors." To end impunity, they note that "current legal frameworks, both statutory and regulatory, need to be reformed and standardised, and other standard-setting frameworks promoted to ensure that the law is actually enforced."

However, since the causes of sexual violence in the universities are "complex, systemic and rooted in social, cultural, economic and institutional dynamics," according to a paper in the Southern African Legal Information Institute (SAFLII), "it is clear that a legal response is only one aspect of an effective strategy. Broad-based preventive measures, institutional strengthening of education systems and staff sensitisation training, public education and awareness raising, and comprehensive victim support services are all essential."

Similar ideas have also been canvassed in Nigeria. On 6 December 2019, the Gender Mobile Initiative (GMI), in partnership with the Ford Foundation, held a 'National Dialogue on Sexual Harassment in Nigerian Tertiary Institutions' in Abuja. In attendance were relevant stakeholders from the academics, development space and regulatory agencies as well as university students. A major highlight of the day were three breakout sessions on the incidences, causes and curative measures of addressing sexual harassment on Nigerian campuses.

Some of the recommendations include the provision of CCTVs across offices and other areas on university campuses as a matter of policy, while restrictions should be placed on meetings between lecturers and their students off campus. Counselling of younger students whose vulnerability can be easily preyed upon by morally decadent lecturers was also proposed, along with stricter enforcement of sanctions against sexual offenders in tertiary institutions. With a call for a lucid definition of what constitutes sexual harassment, regulatory bodies were enjoined to mandate sexual harassment policies as one of the conditions for the accreditation of tertiary institutions, while other authorities in the education sector engage actively in periodic oversight functions and create awareness on the right of students to report abusers and not to suffer in silence.

The GMI Founder/Executive Director, Ms Omowumi Ogunrotimi, whose group has taken its campaign to all Nigerian universities, called for an urgent overhauling of the structure of university education, to instill more accountability in the relationship between the faculties and female students. If we are ever to rid our society of this menace, according to Ogunrotimi, "all stakeholders must stand up to their responsibilities. We must all work to ensure that our campuses are sane, safe and conducive havens for our women and girls to learn without any form of molestation."

Other countries on the continent are also squaring up to the challenge. At its core, sexual harassment is an issue of fundamental human rights not only in the area of education but also "in terms of physical integrity, human dignity, health (physical and mental), freedom from degrading treatment, non-discrimination, justice etc.," according to Dr Melvis Ndiloseh, a Cameroonian senior lecturer and policy analyst. She further observed that the problem "is exacerbated by the acute dearth of institutional policies on sexual harassment and weak enforcement mechanisms, where they exist."

Ndiloseh particularly holds that the manner in which the issue is currently being interrogated on the continent is slightly parochial - as long as the radar remains cast only in the heteronormative mould, with the discussion framed largely around the predatory behaviour of male instructors and administrative authorities towards female students. But while I agree that the gay dimension to the problem is increasingly evident, it is out of the scope of this project. "Although relatively less, this is also a deplorable reality for male students. However, this dimension is more concealed as the male victims tend to be more reticent to speak out. This bit is worth probing along with the attendant implications for youth development," Ndolishe maintained.

Any efforts at broad scoping the menace of sex for grades on the continent, she further argued, "must highlight the many variations of the problem–except, of course, the choice of a homogenous narrative across the board is intentional and justifiable." Above all, as she asserted, "It is high time for institutions of higher learning to divorce blatant denial; acknowledge the facts, forms and prevalence of the problem; and create platforms to collectively brainstorm and map out trajectories for effective prevention and meaningful response. Our schools and universities must be safe spaces for human development, not the albatross of human rights and academic ambitions."

Since the challenge of sex for grades on campuses is not restricted to the continent, the only point that needs to be underscored is that other societies are not in denial, with measures being put in place to tackle it. In the United States, for instance, elimination of sexual harassment is a condition for receiving federal funding for universities, following guidelines to affirm Supreme Court decisions that: "A school can be liable for monetary damages if a teacher sexually harasses a student, an official who has authority to address the harassment has actual knowledge of the harassment and that official is deliberately indifferent in responding to the harassment." This is imperative because: "Preventing and remedying sexual harassment in schools is essential to ensuring a safe environment in which students can learn."

According to Ghanaian academic Fred Awaah, one remedy being explored in parts of Africa is for lecturers not to mark their students' scripts. "In that vein, a lecturer's academic work with a given class should end when his examination has been written. The marking scheme of the given lecturer should be handed over to a different non-predetermined lecturer to mark. The embarrassment associated with informing another lecturer to pass a student, will curb this menace if not totally eradicating it," he wrote in a paper on the so-called sexually transmitted grades.

The Executive Director of the Open Society Initiative for West Africa (OSIWA), Ms Ayisha Osori, who also argues that making the universities more accountable for the general well-being of students under their care is imperative, has slightly different views on this. "There should be full anonymity for the exam scripts so that lecturers do not know who they are grading. This would create more administrative work but the system needs to be designed to remove this bargaining tool from the table," she said.

If we are to change the culture of permissiveness, Osori believes the National Universities Commission (NUC) should "make it a requirement of accreditation that universities have balanced sexual harassment policies that cover students, academic and non-academic staff - complete with grievance procedures, and sharing such policy should be part of orientation for new students." She also calls for clarity on the procedure for managing sexual harassment allegations for all federal and state universities, and the institutions should be defined. "Lecture consultation hours should be set; and it is only outside those hours that lecturers can have their doors closed. CCTV cameras are also another option–in all offices or cover the corridors, so people can see how is going in and out and if doors are being closed despite regulation," she said.

Kenyan Governance expert, Nancy Muigei, suggests that, to tackle the menace effectively, young women need to be empowered to work hard, speak up, organise and mobilise. "There is strength in using their collective power and social media. They need to zealously protect their future. It's challenging now because no measures have been put forward to prevent predators, but their agency and collective action should not be overlooked." Universities across the continent should re-examine their policies and redress measures to ensure they are fit for purpose, she opines. "African Universities need to create safe spaces where young people can raise concerns and their issues investigated and dealt with. Otherwise, we risk leaving behind a productive generation that fails to attain their highest potential because of sexual harassment and exploitation."

It is encouraging that authorities on the continent are now speaking out forcefully against this problem. In Nigeria, the Executive Secretary of the NUC, Prof. Abubakar Rasheed, has on different occasions harped on zero tolerance for sexual harassment, which he said should be vigorously fought on the campuses. "The universities should be willing to punish and stamp out the incidences of sexual harassment because it is damaging to our collective reputation... whenever you punish or sanction somebody in this regard, let your effort be duly publicised. Let the world know that somebody has lost his or her job because of sexual harassment. We can be collecting the names of the offenders monthly and advertising in all the newspapers to expose them as culprits of sexual harassment because we are determined to fight them," Rasheed said at the 33rd annual conference of the Association of Vice Chancellors of Nigerian Universities.

Bemoaning the pervasiveness of the issue of sexual harassment on campuses, the Vice Chancellor of Obafemi Awolowo University, Ile-Ife, Professor Eyitayo Ogunbodede, told me: "You would think that the disgrace Prof Akindele suffered, with the termination of his academic career and the fact that he is currently serving a jail term, would deter others. Sadly, we now have another such allegation in the same faculty. The lecturer is currently being investigated because we believe in due process, but if found guilty, justice will be served."

Ogunbodede informed that, in order to address the challenge more holistically, the university is reviewing its assessment process to go beyond the academic works of the lecturer to issues of character. "We are bringing in external members into that process. No matter how good a lecturer you are, the moment you are identified as someone who abuses your trust with students, you are on your way out of Ife," he declared.

Professor Jacob K. Olupona, Chair of the Committee on African Studies at the Harvard Divinity School, sees the sex for grades phenomenon as "part of a larger national crisis of harassment that cuts across the entire society. It is also part of a culture of oppression of women found everywhere." To address this challenge, Olupona argues that: "The universities should not only put in place a zero tolerance policy on sexual harassment, they must also be proactive and creative in fishing out the culprits. The regular class teaching evaluation of courses must be made compulsory, where the students can comment on their lecturers, including course contents and teaching qualities. One of the questions to ask the students in the evaluation should be a comment on the habits of their lecturers. This is where you give them the chance to comment on their character and attitude to women. These forms should be taken seriously and read by the deans and heads of department before further promotions are made."

The argument in some quarters that female students should also be held to account for the problem, does not hold up to much scrutiny on fiduciary grounds. The university is supposed to be a training ground for young adults to develop mentally and morally before they enter into the larger society. In order for students to attain this level of maturity, according to Abimbola Adelakun of the University of Texas at Austin, "They need the mentorship and relationship that comes with associating with authority figures like professors. It is impractical to ask students not to associate with their professors so that they will not be abused. What the universities need to do is to set the terms and conditions of such relationships. They should prescribe boundaries and ensure they enforce the rules at all times."

She advocates for universities to "take their staff through mandatory and regular trainings on what is appropriate or not, and what constitutes abuse. Some of the professors that have been accused by their students in the past were on their students WhatsApp list, and that is how they are able to chat about issues that have no relevance to their professional relationships and eventually exchange explicit photos. The universities should employ an ethics officer who will regularly train professors on professional boundaries in their informal relationships with their students."

Insisting that lecturers can control themselves, even if students initiate sex - because they are employed to nurture young minds and not treat them as perks of the job - Dr Adelakun observed that the safest measure for any lecturer who does not want to be accused of being an abuser is never to have sex with his students. "People can lie about being abused for different reasons. Relationships that involve an investment of intense emotions get messy, and people can become vindictive. Any professor that does not want to be at the receiving end of that kind of blowback should keep their relationship with their students within professional bounds. Universities should also commit to a judicial process that can resolve abuse of trust with guarantees of transparency, accountability, and a commitment to justice," Adelakun concluded.

Such a redress mechanism, to Ms Dianah Ahumuza of Makerere University's School of Law, "should be reviewed and made more victim-centred and appear impartial. Same applies to the reporting mechanism. Tip-offs should be encouraged. Some of the information can be verified if there is a tip-off Private hotlines for reporting cases with a clearly outlined management process aimed at protecting the victim and encouraging them to come up with evidence to pin the perpetrators."

What is clear is that, in seeking solutions to this challenge, we shouldn't prescribe anything that hinders cordial relationships between lecturers and their students. What should be sought is how to reduce harassment and promote a healthy environment that is void of suspicion and professionally appropriate. A blanket disposition that portrays male lecturers as predatory and female students as temptresses is far from ideal. It is important to understand that we live in societies in which to be accused is to be convicted. Because it is sensational to allege sexual harassment, thoughts should also be spared for the accused, and room left for innocence until proven guilty. Due process should also apportion punishment for flimsy and frivolous claims. The reputation of male lecturers should not be allowed to go into ruin on account of careless and insensitive accusations.

For female undergraduates and policy makers in the education sector on the continent, I concede the last word to Nebila Abdulmelik, a Pan-African and feminist writer from Ethiopia: "We must refuse to accept even what would be considered borderline harassment. We must provide a conducive environment where a survivor can report and be heard and swift action is taken, and where the survivor gets the support, psycho-social and otherwise. If we are to build together, not only the Africa we want, but more fundamentally, the Africa we need - for ourselves as well as coming generations, we must do better as a people."

PART TWO

A 'VACCINE' FOR
THE SHADOW PANDEMIC

Sexual harassment is really not about sex. It's about power and aggression and manipulation. It's an abuse of power problem.

– PROF. JAMES CAMPBELL QUICK,

University of Texas at Arlington

PREFACE

On 9th September 2020, Obafemi Awolowo University (OAU), Ile-Ife hosted a Webinar with the theme, 'Finding safe spaces for female students in Nigerian universities'. Notable speakers at the four-hour session included Vice President Yemi Osinbajo, SAN, GCON, the Deputy Senate President, Senator Ovie Omo-Agege, the 14th Emir of Kano, HRH Muhammadu Sanusi II, First Lady of Ekiti State, Erelu Bisi Adeleye-Fayemi, Secretary General, Women Rights Advancement and Protection Alternative (WRAPA), Hajiya Saudatu Mahdi and Director, West Africa Office, Ford Foundation, Mr Innocent Chukwuma. Other speakers were Prof. Joy Ezeilo of the University of Nigeria, Nsukka, President of the Queens College, Lagos Alumni, Mrs Ifueko Omoigui Okuaru, former Head of Service of the Federation, Mr Steve Oronsaye, Lagos lawyer, Adeyinka Olumide-Fusika, SAN as well as Dr Okey Ikechukwu, Ms Ebunoluwa Adejuyigbe and the Special Adviser to Ekiti State Governor on Basic Education, Prof. Francisca Aladejano. The Director, Centre for Gender and Social Policy Studies, Dr Monica Orisadare worked with the chairperson, OAU Investment Company, Prof Funmi Soetan to coordinate the Webinar.

In welcoming participants to the Webinar, the moderator, Prof Oluyemisi Obilade highlighted some of the efforts that have been made in the past few years to address the issue of sexual harassment that has impacted negatively on many of the young women who have passed through Nigerian universities. The difference between the past and the present, Obilade added, is that the veil of silence is gradually being removed with the issue now in the public arena.

The chief host, the OAU Vice Chancellor, Prof. Eyitayo Ogunbodede explained why addressing the issue of sexual harassment was crucial to the development of the nation. The gender dimension to the acquisition of knowledge in a campus environment, according to Ogunbodede, must be given critical attention because girls and women are vulnerable to factors which discourage qualitative learning such as discrimination and sexual violence. Prof Funmi Soetan amplified Ogunbodede's argument by saying that the challenge of sexual violence is not restricted to the campus, essentially because it is enabled by unequal power dynamics.

Sex for grade, according to Prof Soetan, is an oppressive form of gender inequality which violates not only the rights of women but also robs them of their dignity while the fear of retaliation, stigmatization, victim blaming and a weak enforcement mechanism combine to aid sexual harassment in institutions of higher learning. Sexual violence, whether on campus or within the larger society, Prof Soetan argued, could be physical, emotional or psychological and it includes "threats of such act and coercion or arbitrary deprivation of liberty whether occurring in private or public life."

In his goodwill message, the National Universities Commission (NUC) Executive Secretary, Professor Abubakar Adamu Rasheed, said he found it disheartening to read some words and phrases thrown up in the book, 'NAKED ABUSE:

Sex for grades in African Universities' because they "negate everything that a university stands for and should, therefore, not be heard in its community." The NUC, said Rasheed, "remains committed to ensuring the delivery of quality tertiary education in an environment that is safe, secure and conducive for everyone, especially the students, who are the reason universities exist." He added that he has noted the suggestions made in the book. "With many Universities in the country already embracing and domesticating the Sexual Harassment Policy, NUC will continue to work in partnership with well-meaning individuals and organisations to curb sexual exploitation in any form in our institutions of higher learning," Rasheed said.

Investigative journalist, Ms Kiki Mordi, whose expose on some lecturers in Nigerian and Ghanaian Universities who harass female students (aired on the British Broadcasting Corporation (BBC)), helped to put global focus on the menace, also sent a goodwill message. With the menace of sexual violence on the campuses of institutons of higher learning now in the forefront of public discourse, according to Mordi, stakeholders can now choose on which side of history they want to belong. Special Adviser to the Ekiti State Governor on Basic Education, Prof Fancesca Aladejana argued that the society must find a way to educate our men in the knowledge sector, including in primary and secondary schools, on the need to exercise self-discipline. "They should understand that the authority they have over female students, or any student at all, comes with enormous responsibility," said Aladejana.

With 395 active participants, notable personalities who attended the Webinar included the Governor of Kwara State, Mr Abdulraham Abdulrazaq, former Governor of Cross River State, Mr Donald Duke, former Director General, Bureau of Public Procurement (BPP), Eng. Emeka Ezeh, Chairman,

Caverton Group, Mr Remi Makanjuola, retired Judge of the Federal High Court, Justice Mojisola Olatoregun and Chairman, National Salaries, Income and Wages Commission (NSIWC) Mr Ekpo Nta, who as ICPC Chairman started to beam searchlight on university lecturers who abuse their trust.

Also in attendance were the Executive Secretary, Nigeria Extractive Industries Transparency Initiative (NEITI), Mr Waziri Adio, former Youth and Sports Minister, Mallam Bolaji Abdullahi and Chairman of Phase 3 Telecoms, Mr Stanley Jegede. THISDAY Managing Director, Mr Eniola Bello and his deputy, Comrade Kayode Komolafe as well as the ICPC Director of Legal, Mr Adenekan Sogunle. Amnesty International Niger Direcor, Mr Osai Ojigbo, Prof Musbau Akanji of the University of Ilorin, Dr Ngozi Azodoh of the Federal Ministry of Health and Hajia Ramatu Ibrahim of Pure Garment also attended.

With participants drawn from United States, United Kingdom, Canada, Hungary and Nigeria, the Director, Women Advocates and Research and Documentation Centre (WARDC), Dr Abiola Akiyode and the president/CEO of Beloxxi Industries Limited, Dr Obi Ezeude also attended along with several others, including the Chief of Staff to the Deputy Senate President, Mr Otive Igbuzor, as well as Mrs Olayinka Fagbenro of the National Space Research and Development Agency (NASRDA)and Hajiya Raheemat Momodu of the ECOWAS Secretariat, Abuja.

The chairman, Brooks&Blade, Ms. Funmi Onajide, Harvard Professor, Jacob Olupona, Father George Ehusani, Ms Ifeoma Ngozi Malo, Dr Chidi Amuta, Brig-Gen. Mustapha Onoyiveta (rtd), Mr Feyi Fayehinmi (Aguntasolo), Sister Tina Chikezie and several others were also in attendance.

In the following pages, I bring to readers some of the major interventions at the Webinar.

(Female) students are vulnerable because male lecturers are in a position of power and they (female students) might feel flattered when a (male) lecturer shows interest in them.

– AMANDA GOUWS, professor of political science,
University of Stellenbosch, South Africa.

CHAPTER FIVE

HOW WE SHOULD
FIGHT THE MENACE

EYITOPE OGUNBODEDE

Excerpts from the welcome remarks by the Vice Chancellor of Obafemi
Awolowo University, Ile-Ife, the chief host of the Webinar

The education of girls and women has always been of
global interest because it promotes individual and national
well-being, increases the chances for income generation and
is tied to the quality of life of future generations. Learning
is enhanced through the creation and maintenance of a
conducive environment and an atmosphere which promotes
critical thinking, innovation, skills acquisition and sustained
assimilation. The gender dimension of learning must therefore
be given critical attention, because girls and women are
vulnerable to factors which demotivate them and discourage
qualitative learning, such as a toxic environment characterized
by victimization, intimidation, sexual harassment and sexual
violence.

The workings of all sector of the society including the

educational sector requires concerted efforts from the political, economic and social segments. Policies and frameworks are important in maintaining order and ensuring the safety of learners. It is at this point that I must commend the 9th National Assembly on the passage of the anti-sexual harassment bill, sponsored by Senator Ovie Omo-Agege whom we have in attendance today. This Bill will enhance the creation of a safe environment for the delivery of quality education. It is a thing of great relief to know that our leaders care about the safety of the learning environment and the physical, emotional and mental well-being of the learners.

As we are all aware, there has been what the United Nation's Secretary General, Mr. Antonio Guterres has referred to as a shadow pandemic, the increase in cases of violence against women just as the global COVID-19 pandemic was also ravaging the world. If the human race suddenly confronted with a novel deadly virus can swiftly mobilise resources to create a vaccine that will save the lives of many going forward, surely it can also commit rigorously to create a vaccine that can reduce, to the barest minimum, a pandemic that has diminished the quality of life of millions of women and girls the world over – Violence Against Women. More so, this menace is not novel at all, it has been in existence for many years and it continues to destroy societies. We must therefore consider the task of securing the lives of half of the world's population as though we were responding to a contemporary terrorist attack.

The Obafemi Awolowo University (OAU) as a matter of policy has ZERO TOLERANCE for any form of sexual harassment. And there are mechanisms in place to ensure strict conformity. I am happy to inform you that OAU has a robust Anti Sexual Harassment (ASH) policy. In addition, there is an ASH implementation Committee headed by Professor

(Mrs) Olateju, supported by Faculty and Departmental ASH Committees to ensure proper compliance and monitoring of the policy. Also the University through its various arms especially the Centre for Gender and Social Policy Studies (headed by Dr. Monica Orisadare) continuously carry out research to update knowledge on Sexual Harassment issues in the society. For instance, there is an ongoing project on Anti Sexual Harassment initiated by OAU and extending to other Nigerian Universities. An App is also being developed for monitoring and collating information on Sexual Harassment. The university also recently played host to the shooting of CITATION, a movie produced by Kunle Afolayan which narrates the ordeals faced by a female postgraduate student (acted by Temi Otedola) who is forced to find a way to deal with a situation of sexual harassment from a male lecturer.

The cast includes Dr. Ibukun Awosika (Chairman of First Bank) an Alumna of OAU who played the role of a Faculty Dean and Chairman of the Senate Investigative Panel. The choice of OAU as the site for the shooting of the movie was based on our strong Anti-Sexual-Harassment policy and the endowment of OAU as Africa's most beautiful University campus. These efforts by OAU are all in a bid to address the menace of Sexual Harassment and create a safe learning environment for all. The University through the Centre for Gender and Social Policy Studies continuously look forward to your support and collaboration in combating this societal menace.

When some weeks ago our distinguished Alumnus and Guest Speaker at this Webinar, Olusegun Adeniyi, informed me that he would like to donate copies of his latest book, 'NAKED ABUSE' to OAU, I immediately capitalised on the opportunity to request that he should please go "another mile" by supporting the University to organise a Webinar on anti-sexual harassment. I was convinced that OAU would benefit immensely from the rich experience and global outlook that he powerfully portrayed in 'NAKED ABUSE'. I find the book highly captivating and grounded in current realities of sexual harassment and sexual violence in Nigerian and other African Universities.

Thankfully, this Webinar is a 'vaccine' that we can use to tackle the menace of sexual violence on our campuses. It will, no doubt, further illuminate our minds on effective ways to ensure that our tertiary institutions are safe spaces for every learner, especially women. It will enable us to re-position the educational sector and contribute concretely to transforming the lives of students and to nation building. I look forward to a very exciting and highly productive Webinar. We should take the lessons from the lectures, keynote speeches and panel discussion and inject them into every sphere of influence as Safe Space Ambassadors. It is our hope that this kind of effort would enable universities in Nigeria, Africa and the world benefit maximally from quality education delivered in highly secured and safe environment, devoid of any form of sexual harassment or violence.

CHAPTER SIX

WE NEED A
WHISTLEBLOWER PROCESS

YEMI OSINBAJO

Transcript of the keynote remarks by the vice president,
Prof Yemi Osinbajo, SAN, GCON, at the Webinar

We all owe a debt of gratitude to the Obafemi Awolowo University for providing the platform for this important conversation on 'Finding Safe Spaces for Female Students in Nigerian Universities' and for the kind invitation to make a few remarks at this webinar. I am also grateful to my brother, Olusegun Adeniyi who insisted on my participation at this webinar. His book, "Naked Abuse sex for grades in African Universities", a researched work sponsored by the Ford Foundation is, as the vice-chancellor has pointed out, one of the main inspirations for this webinar.

I must confess that because of the extremely readable style that he adopts, I was almost grateful that this research was not done by an academic like myself (apologies to my fellow professors), we would have ended up with volumes of very difficult to read the material. So, I think that Segun has, in a few pages, done an excellent job of not just confronting us with the key issues in the sordid situations of sex for grades on the African Continent but he has also made several important suggestions on what to do and how to solve the problem.

Let me begin by saying that for me as an academic and a lawyer, I am always mindful of the need to define as well as possible, what the problem is. And I think that is where I just like to start, by understanding the definition of the words that we use, and of course the definition of this particular problem. It was the Association of Women Judges who, in a tool kit which they published very recently, described this problem as 'Sextortion'. I think it is an important definition because it clearly puts in perspective what we should be thinking about and what the elements are.

The definition as they described it as "The abuse of power to obtain a sexual favour or advantage", or to borrow further from them, they say that, in effect, "Sextortion is a form of corruption in which sex, rather than money, is the currency of the bribe." I think the definition is helpful because it also helps us to shape the legal theory under which the conduct itself can be dealt with.

Evidently, under Nigerian law, and I think that the Deputy Senate President has already covered a fair amount of the description of this offence under Nigerian law. But I think the offence could fit into well-established categories. Of course, it can qualify as an act of corruption. And as Segun points out in his book, the successful prosecution of Professor Akindele (of the University of Ife) was done by the ICPC. And the ICPC based its prosecution on the definition of corruption in the Act. What you need to prove in such a case, is that a person in a position of authority demanded gratification (this is wide enough definition to cover demand for sex) in exchange for a benefit, in this case, good grades.

So, by definition, it is an act of corruption and it could qualify easily as an act of corruption, and it could also qualify, as has been pointed out as rape or attempted rape. The definition of rape under our law is having sex with a woman without her consent or where the consent was obtained by threats or intimidation of any kind. That is very important here because demand for sex with a choice of failure or success in an examination will qualify as a threat or intimidation. By the way, punishment for rape is life imprisonment while attempted rape is 14-year imprisonment, so even the punishment is very severe. And a more all-encompassing definition of rape and other forms of violence is contained in the Violence against Persons Act which was referred to, again, by the distinguished Deputy Senate President.

Various iterations of that law are now domesticated in several states. But I agree with the DSP that there is still a need for a sexual harassment specific bill because there are still various contours of sexual harassment that are not covered by the established definitions of corruption or rape under our laws in the south or the penal code in the north. So, I think that a sexual harassment specific legislation is one that is still desirable.

I believe our search for answers to creating safe spaces for female students in our universities must begin from the question of why is it that such an evidently rampant crime is so under-reported. There are obviously many cases of people who share their anecdotal experiences without necessarily reporting to the authorities. I think the answer is clearly that this low reportability is on account of the fact that many victims do not feel confident that they will get redress, or that they will be treated fairly or that they will not be visited with the same fearful consequences that was the subject of the demand in the first place. The fear that they will neither get a sympathetic nor understanding hearing, let alone justice, and that they will end up suffering the same consequences the predator had threatened would occur if they did not submit to their demands. Then there is, of course, the shame and stigma that could attend speaking up.

So, I think that in ensuring that we create safe spaces, we must do at least the basics, which is providing the support and resources they need to report abusers. Every institution must make it easy for victims or potential victims to report perpetrators to trusted formal structures or secure channels created specifically for the purpose of resolving such cases. And I think it should be made very clear. Every institution ought to say, "We have this structure and it is accessible to every student".

A well-thought-out whistleblower process emphasizing confidentiality and professional legal and medical help for victims or potential victims should be mandatory. Aside from victims, whistleblowers should also, under a properly designed scheme, should be able to advance information that they have, and in appropriate cases, professional legal and medical help for victims should also be provided.

To ensure that both faculty and students are sufficiently clear about the issues and rules, there is a need for codes of conduct or ethical guidelines based on best practices in appropriate student/lecturer interactions. It is important that these are clearly defined in ethical guidelines that are contained in some documents that people can refer to and see. It is important both for the lecturer and the student that there is some reference to some code of conduct.

Segun, in his book, notes the practice, I believe is in Makerere University where, as an ethical guideline, consultations between students and lecturers must be done with doors open and meetings cannot be held outside of the faculty premises. Meetings elsewhere would raise a presumption of wrongdoing (If I call a meeting to discuss a dissertation or a term paper with a student and I picked a hotel as a conducive environment for doing that, it could raise a presumption of wrongdoing). The clarity that attends these sorts of conduct and the ethical rules that must be abided by will greatly help in creating a much safer environment for our female students.

The other conceptual problem with offences of this nature is where the fault might be located. But there is sometimes the point that is made that victims might have brought the offence upon themselves by their attitude, dress or willingness to be in a compromising place with the lecturer, and this is one notion that must be resisted. The victim must always be seen as the victim. There cannot be an excuse especially given the power configuration between students and lecturers that the victim could have somehow invited the abuse upon themselves. I think it is an important consideration to be made and we must not allow that notion to persist.

There is also the comparison sometimes made between demanding bribes for service and sex for grades. Sometimes people will argue that a bribe is a bribe and there is no reason why the punishment for sex as the currency of the bribe, should be stricter than an ordinary bribe.

I think that the two are vastly different and they have vastly different impacts on the victim. Loss of cash in payment of a bribe is vastly different (in my view) from the physical violation and the lingering shame, guilt and other psychological effects that the violation will visit on the victim especially a young person. I think the psychological effects are long-running, and the DSP has also made the point about the lingering psychological effects and this sort of devastation may never heal.

So, clearly, the offender should be visited with the strictest possible consequences.

Let me say in conclusion that we must stay engaged on this issue, governments and civil society. We are extremely proud of the work the DSP has done on the bill and the very determined way in which he has continued to pursue it. I think that we must all become champions of creating a safe environment for females in our universities. The easier it is to report cases, the easier it is to be heard with empathy and assurance of redress in appropriate cases, the faster the eradication or at least reduction of this reprehensible phenomenon will be.

CHAPTER SEVEN

THE MISCHIEF WE MUST CURE

OVIE OMO-AGEGE

Keynote speech at the Webinar by the Deputy Senate President whose bill on sexual harassment was finally passed by the 9th Senate in April 2020 after a four-year effort, beginning from the 8th Senate

My intervention here today is focused mainly on the need for the Sexual Harassment of Students in Tertiary Educational Institutions (Prohibition) Bill, 2019 (Senate Bill (SB) 77), which I am privileged to sponsor with the support of virtually all my colleagues. The Bill was recently passed with unanimous consent in the Senate. It is now in the House of Representatives for further legislative action. But please permit me to situate my intervention within the context of the succinct statement of the history of sexual harassment as culled from an article in the 'Law Journal BD' as follows:

> *"The term 'sexual harassment' first came into use in the late 1970s in the United States. The term's origins are generally traced to a course on women and work taught by Lin Farley at Cornell University. In 1979, Catherine MacKinnon, a legal scholar from the United States, made the first argument that*

sexual harassment is a form of sex discrimination prohibited by the constitution and civil rights laws of the United States. Since then many international bodies, national legislatures and courts have prohibited sexual harassment but have not agreed on a universal definition of the term.

"The United Nations General Recommendation 19 to the 'Convention on the Elimination of all Forms of Discrimination Against Women' reaffirms these elements by defining sexual harassment to include 'such unwelcome sexually determined behavior as physical contact and advances, sexually colored remarks, showing pornography and sexual demands, whether by words or actions'."

The Bill is an attempt by the National Assembly to align Nigeria with the comity of nations in dealing decisively with sexual harassment in our tertiary educational institutions. Let me quickly provide some reported cases and perspectives in Nigeria as an added context to sexual predation on our campuses:

- On 27th November 1988, the editorial of the *SUNDAY TRIBUNE* stated in part that: 'Sexual harassment is rampant in all Nigerian institutions of higher learning. In some places, it has almost become an accepted fact that the female student must submit.'

- In 2013, the National Universities Commission (NUC) stated in a report that, 'Sexual harassment seems to rank extremely very high among corrupt practices uncovered in our universities."

- In 2014, the International Journal of Applied Psychology noted that:

    "... [I]n Nigeria, sex for grades in tertiary institutions is a reality and the male lecturers in particular, perceive themselves as thin (sic) gods and such unprofessional behaviour can be perpetuated unchecked."

- In 2016, the *VANGUARD* published that: "... [O]ur campuses of supposed higher learning are more or less veritable sexual jungles where academic staff ... are prowling predators. Sex for marks or other favours has become so entrenched as to have acquired the status of a law of nature. Put bluntly, it is as if our university, polytechnic and college of education campuses are sex colonies where rape or any other form of coerced copulation and intimacy may be practised without sanctions... Always, the sex-obsessed lecturer wielding his illegitimate power asks drily: Do you want to pass this course to graduate, or not?"

- Not long ago, the world was shocked when the British Broadcasting Corporation (BBC) aired a shameful tale of a supposed pastor and lecturer, who allegedly abused his office for sexual gains.

- Many female students, including a Miss Shola of University of Ibadan (as reported by *VANGUARD*), Hamzat Kaothar of University of Abuja, and Chinelo Emenike of Imo State University (as reported by (*PREMIUM TIMES*), have been prevented from graduating on time because they were brazenly victimized for daring to reject amoral advances by lecturers.

- In all of these, Dr. Adekunle Idris, a former Chairman of ASUU at the Lagos State University (*PREMIUM TIMES*) admitted with courageous frankness that: *"The truth of the matter is for now we don't have specific guidance in respect to sanctions (for sexual harassment of students). What we are doing is to continually sensitise our members ... to ensure that best practises are always adhered ... It is only a matter of moral suasion ..."*

This distressing chronicle of sexual harassment, impunity and predation on our campuses has spurred the National Assembly to action. As a parent, I am appalled by these happenings. This indecency does not represent our values as a people. As a Senator of the Federal Republic, I refuse to allow this pandemic to ruin our academic standards or define and destroy the reputation of the great majority of decent academics on our campuses. This is the main reason why I introduced the Sexual Harassment (Prohibition) Bill, first in 2016 and again in 2019.

Undoubtedly, the scourge of sexual harassment with its repugnant subculture of sex-for-grades in our tertiary institutions is an extraordinary mischief impacting negatively on our educational standards. Permit me to echo the succinct statement from the article in the Law Journal BD:

> *"American scholars maintain that "sexual harassment often has a serious and negative impact on women's physical and emotional health, and the more severe the harassment, the more severe the reaction. The reactions frequently reported by women include anxiety, depression, sleep disturbance, weight loss or gain, loss of appetite, and headaches. Researchers have also found that there is a link between sexual harassment and Post-Traumatic Stress Disorder."*

The foregoing really underscores the debilitating impact of sexual harassment and how it impairs the standard and quality of education in our tertiary educational institutions. Item 60(e) of the Exclusive Legislative List of the Constitution of the Federal Republic of Nigeria, 1999 (as altered) specifically empowers the National Assembly to make laws "prescribing minimum standards of education". Sexual harassment on our campuses is a hideous attack on our educational standards and the Bill is sponsored to stop it. Indeed, the Bill (SB77) seeks to protect the right of students to learn peaceably without any form of sexual harassment. This is supported by section 45(1) of the Constitution which says, "(1) Nothing in sections

37, 38, 39 and 40 ... of this Constitution shall invalidate any law that is reasonably justifiable in a democratic society ... (b) for the purpose of protecting the rights and freedom of other persons".

Giving judicial imprimatur to the legislative power of the National Assembly, the Supreme Court in ATTORNEY GENERAL OF ONDO STATE V ATTORNEY GENERAL OF THE FEDERATION [2002] NWLR (PT 772) 222 Per UWAIFO, J.S.C. at pages 408-409, paragraphs H-C, held that:

> "... [T]here may be occasion, and probably always would, when what appears a local problem assumes such a proportion as to become a matter of concern to a federal country as a whole. In such a case it may turn out to be inevitable to regard the matter as affecting the peace, order and good government of the country which ought to be so addressed by means of a uniform law."

CASE FOR THE BILL

In sponsoring this Bill, we are not unmindful of some legislations dealing with various forms of sexual assaults. Section 282 to 285 of the Penal Code covers some of these offences, including "Rape and Unnatural and Indecent Offences" in the Northern part of the country. Similarly, section 357 to 363 of the Criminal Code deals with related offences in the Southern part of the country under the heading of "Assaults on Females". There is also the Violence Against Persons (Prohibition) (VAPP) Act, 2015 which has now been domesticated in at least 13 States including Lagos, Oyo, Ogun, Osun, Ekiti, Edo, Anambra, Enugu, Ebonyi, Benue, Cross River, Kaduna, and Plateau. Amongst others, the VAPP Act rightly defines rape much more broadly than the Codes. It provides stiffer penalties for offences against a person's body, including gang rape and incest. The Act established the Sex Offenders' Register as a major innovation. There is also the Child Rights Act which forbids sex with a child – same being statutory rape. It has been domesticated in about 25 States.

The Bill is a critical component in the fight against sexual harassment, particularly as there is growing recognition of sexual harassment as a form of violence against women. States are obligated under international law to take effective steps to protect women from violence and to hold harassers and/or their employers accountable for sexual harassment in the workplace.

Generally, a victim's informed and voluntary consent is a defence to a charge of rape and some other sex-related offences under the Criminal and Penal Codes and the VAPP Act. But consent is no defence if the victim is a minor. The very act (actus reus) proves the crime, without more. The prosecutor has no burden to prove the guilty mind (mens rea) of the suspect. This is statutory rape for which strict liability attaches. Significantly, from a strictly technical perspective, these extant legislations do not properly cover 'sexual harassment' though it is recognised globally as a distinct species of sexual offence. Many alleged offenders have gotten away with rape and sexual harassment on the pretext of consent by their victims.

This raises a fundamental question of whether the defence of informed and voluntary consent to the charge of rape or sexual harassment should apply in relation to a student victim given the UNIQUE and IMBALANCED nature of the student-educator relationship of AUTHORITY, DEPENDENCY and TRUST. On this, the Senate has carefully considered and determined that based on the legal principle of in loco parentis, sexual harassment of students by any educator qualifies as statutory rape to which strict liability must attach. This is exactly what we have done by passing the Bill unanimously. But I should add that the Bill does not deal with only making carnal knowledge of a student by an educator a strict liability offence. It comprehends sexual harassment in all its manifestations and imposes strict liability penal sanctions on the harasser.

By the in loco parentis principle, the law confers a quasi-parental status on the educator and recognises his/her fiduciary authority over the student. Conversely, the student depends on the educator for career development for a better future. Inherent in this view is the fact that the student infinitely trusts the educator like a good parent to protect her/his best interest always. The law does not expect the educator to exploit this relationship for direct or indirect benefits at the expense of the student's proper development.

Like a minor, a student is vulnerable in the student-educator relationship, irrespective of age. If a predator lecturer exploits this vulnerability beneficially, that reprehensible act itself must be penalised with or without consent, as there cannot be informed and voluntary consent by a student who is held hostage by an educator. By removing mutual consent between the student and educator as a defence, this Bill defines any proven act of sexual harassment as a strict liability offence.

The uniqueness of the student-educator relationship is the predicate of all laws prohibiting sexual harassment in tertiary institutions globally. Nigeria has chosen to be part of this positive trend to protect our students. We cannot by indifference or complacency allow this relationship to be abused without consequences in Nigeria.

'TARGETING' EDUCATORS

Our legislative leadership on this pandemic has been mischaracterised by some as an unfriendly act against our educators. We reject that misrepresentation. It is entirely false. We have no reason whatsoever to fight our lecturers and teachers who nurtured some of us to become the leaders that we are today. On the contrary, the Bill is a child of necessity to stop sexual predators on our campuses. It is meant to rid our educational community of sexual harassers, while protecting the good reputation of the vast majority of our educators who are not sexual predators.

Indeed, there is nothing new about enacting a law specifically against sexual harassment in tertiary institutions. On this point, I respectfully cite a few global examples:

- In America, the Honour Code, Title 7 of the Civil Rights Act of 1964 and Title 9 of the Higher Education Amendments Act of 1972 prohibit sexual harassment of students in tertiary institutions by faculty members, and it is a criminal offence to violate these instruments;
- In the United Kingdom, it is a serious crime under sections 16 – 24 of the Sexual Offenses Act ,2003 for a person in the position off an educator to exploit the student-educator relationship for sexual benefit because, it is a relationship where there is an IMBALANCE of POWER and RESPONSIBILITY;
- In Queensland, Australia, the law also expressly forbids sexual intimacy and sexual harassment in the student-educator relationship;
- In South Africa, it is an offence under Section 17 of the Employment of Educators Act, 1998 (as amended) for an educator to have a sexual relationship with a student; and
- In fact, 2018 World Bank Group's Women (Business

and the Law) data show that several African countries have laws that specifically penalize sexual harassment in educational institutions.

Clearly, the countries mentioned above designed and fitted their laws against sexual harassment of students to where the problem is – the academic institutions. This does not mean that laws cannot be made for other sectors of society where a similar mischief rises to the level of repugnancy now pervading on our campuses. In any case, the Constitution expressly grants the National Assembly the authority to act firmly to protect our standards of education and pass laws for the order peace and good governance of Nigeria.

Sexual Harassment in our tertiary educational institution is a national problem that requires a uniform national response to combat and eliminate in every tertiary educational institution in any part of the country. We will not shirk that solemn duty.

When people realize that all women are at risk for sexual assault, survivors are less likely to be left on their own.

– JULIENNE LUSENGE, Journalist and female activist, Democratic Republic of the Congo (DRC)

CHAPTER EIGHT

A TIMELY CONVERSATION

MUHAMMADU SANUSI II

The 14th Emir of Kano wades in on what stakeholders must continue to do

It is a great pleasure and honour for me to make a goodwill remark at this very important Webinar on finding safe spaces for female students in Nigeria universities. Let me begin by thanking Olusegun Adeniyi for the great work he's done and also highlight the fact that the threat to female university students goes beyond sexual abuse and harassment by academics to abuse and harassment by fellow students.

Besides, they are also victims of the general insecurity in our environment. So, perhaps the first thing to ask for is that how we treat and protect our women should be brought to the forefront of national discourse. Women, the girl child and female students need to be protected from rape, violence and all forms of abuse. And we need to properly define what constitutes harassment, what constitutes abuse so as to ensure that our children, our sisters are able to go to Nigerian universities and can compete along with their fellow male students without being conscious of their gender and sexuality.

This is therefore an extremely important conversation.

Once more I congratulate Segun and I thank those who have taken the time to participate in this conference especially the vice president and the deputy senate president and I thank the university for providing this platform for our voices to be joined with all their voices in the call to ensure that our students are safe and that they are able to flourish in the university environment and compete with students anywhere in the world.

THERE MUST BE ZERO TOLERANCE

INNOCENT CHUKWUMA

The Regional Director, West Africa, Ford Foundation speaks on why there should be no tolerance for all manners of sexual abuse on the campuses

I welcome the opportunity to participate in this important webinar on finding safe spaces for female students in Nigerian Universities. I particularly congratulate and thank the OAU for the courage and leadership it has displayed in hosting this seminar. This is because, in crime and criminal justice, what increases peoples' perception of safety and security in a place is not necessarily the absence of crime, criminality and other infractions. It is often the type and effectiveness of the response that is initiated whenever such incidents occur and how it is communicated to send the message of zero tolerance that goes a long way in reassuring people that they are protected.

The Obafemi Awolowo University has distinguished itself and demonstrated these in its response to the recent event in the University, especially how the authorities came out to fully investigate it, ensured that the culprit had his day in court where he was convicted and in leading the current efforts to ensure that our universities are indeed safe spaces for learning for all our students, especially female students.

Ford Foundation has been a long standing partner of the global women rights movement in its efforts to ensure that our campuses, workplaces, public spaces and homes are safe for women and girls. In 2018, the West Africa office under my leadership chose to revise our program areas to prioritize work on Ford's international Gender, Racial and Ethnic Justice (GREJ) program, which is explicitly focused on ending violence against women and girls (VAWG). We strongly believe that supporting VAWG organizations, especially those working to tackle violence against women and girls, is the most effective mechanism for ensuring sustainable change in the lives of women and girls and currently 71% of annual grantmaking goes to leading women rights and women led organizations in the region and reflects this commitment.

Our current strategy for addressing VAWG in West Africa, and particularly in Nigeria, is focused on holding authorities, including religious, traditional leaders, heads of public and private institutions, accountable for violence against women in their domains. So, the era of hiding under social norms, cultures and traditions to tolerate and perpetuate the worst forms of violence and abuse against women and girls is nearing its end. We should not tolerate and allow it to continue to happen in our society.

Permit me to stress that the Ford Foundation also support institutions and individuals outside the feminist and women rights movement who wield some influence on the media, policy circles and other important sectors to lend their voices and support to the efforts of women rights movement to end VAWG in our society. This is because of the need to widen the space of actors working in this field and our belief that bringing together various groups working on the issue to partner with one another will contribute in inching us towards a day when our universities, public spaces, public and private sectors would be reed of violence against women.

The Vice Chancellor earlier spoke glowingly about the film Kunle Afolayan made on sexual harassment on university campuses in West Africa, including Nigeria. It might interest the audience to know that Ford Foundation supported the production of the film, which I believe would soon be on Netflix to ensure wider distribution. We've also supported the ICPC to strengthen its Unit responsible for investigating sexual corruption in the public sector, including the Universities. Last but certainly not the least is our support for Olusegun Adeniyi's latest book, titled 'NAKED ABUSE', which threw a searchlight on Sex for grades in African universities and I believe, influenced the organization of this important seminar.

In closing, I cannot help but underscore the point the Vice President, Prof. Yemi Osinbajo, made in his keynote speech, which is that, in all that we do both as insiders and outsiders in the advocacy to end violence against women and girls, we should not fail to centre the victims. Victims blaming should be condemned in all its entirety because in our society, we have seen infants and minors being defiled sexualy abused and harassed and the question is what role could they have played in aiding the perpetrators? Victim of sexual abuse go through dificult times before deciding to come out and need all the support that we can muster to ensure that they get justice.

There is a pattern to close ranks, admit nothing and blame the victim.

– DR BRADY WILSON,

a psychologist in Scottsdale, Arizona

THE QUESTIONS WE
MUST ADDRESS

IFUEKO OMOIGUI OKAURU

Former Chair of the Federal Inland Revenue Service (FIRS) and President of the
Queen's College Old Girls Association raises three questions

Just as has been said by previous speakers, there are a lot of steps to be taken if we are to effectively address this problem. I must say that, the more people speak up and write about the realities of what is going on, the better for all of us. I also like to note that the issue os beyond tertiary institutions. We should start much earlier at the primary and secondary institutions (and also address issues in the home) as part of the plan to improve tertiary institutions. I have three questions and or comments.

One, how do we encourage people to speak up and take action especially those who are in the vanguard of the change we desire in this area?

I have a recent example of an activist who had an opportunity to report a personal case but hesitated to do so, claiming that "people do these things, and so nothing can be done about it". We need more role models who can give courage to others to speak up. When we have activists who people know have such experiences, and they themselves are reluctant to speak up and take action, it weakens the resolve of others or tampers with their belief that something can be done. We should speak up and be ready to take the next step to do something about this so that the consequences of harassment, assault and rape help mitigate the risks of reoccurrence

Two, beyond putting a law in place, laws, particularly at government level for government schools where the laws may not be in focus, there is a need to put policies and directives in place to guide action at the school level. Ministries at the Federal and at the State level should have well defined policies and directives that have clear consequences and protocols. I believe there is a gap there. I am very happy to hear what UNN has done in championing not just policy, but the actions taken to bring policy to life.

How do we bridge the need for policies and directives in primary, secondary and tertiary institutions that can be acted upon? How do we have peer learning and share experiences on a regular basis? People get strength from what others have done as it answers the question, how do we really do all these?

Three has to do with the building of trust development of character. Trust doesn't just happen. Character is developed and taught. Let us not assume that people understand how to be trustworthy.

How do we devote resources to building character? There are a lot of resources to building character. ReStraL Ltd, the company I chair has programs for teacher development at all levels. We can aspire to develop the kind of teachers we need through training and retraining as well as how we manage their performance on a periodic basis. We are clearer on our expectations of our teachers and academics in the strictly academic fields, but we spend less focus on developing character as a critical part of learning.

We should also provide the necessary funding to do this. This is a call to Government, the Private Sector and NGOs to support character development. They should also please work with the Alumni.

There is always a power differential and that power differential [puts] someone at high risk to lose a job, to fail a course, to not get a job, or to not get a letter of recommendation…So, in making a report, they always do so…at a personal risk to themselves, professionally or educationally.

– SAUNDRA SCHUSTER,
Partner with the National Center for Higher Education Risk Management (NCHERM), a consulting firm in the United States

WHAT IT DOES TO VICTIMS

MONICA ORISADARE

The Director, OAU Centre for Gender and Social Policy Studies, speaks to
what sexual violence does to female students on the campuses

Let me express our sincere gratitude to all our invited speakers who have taken the time out of their busy schedules to contribute their thoughts towards the cause of eradicating sexual violence against female students. Indeed, as the guest speaker has submitted, our voices matter because we each have a role to play in ensuring that violence towards and intimidation of female students is not proliferated and normalized in our learning institutions.

As the lead and principal representative at the Centre for Gender and Social Policy Studies, Obafemi Awolowo University, I want to state here that we are committed to upholding the legal and institutional frameworks which have been provided to ensure the safety of learners, especially women. We recognise that education delivers so much value in the lives of women. It increases the chances of them being employed and earning an income, it promotes good decision making in terms of child bearing, child spacing and raising children who have better chances of surviving infancy and attending schools. The education of women is the key to a vibrant future for societies and nations because when girls and women are educated, societies, communities and nations practically receive the mental empowerment needed for a life of productivity, impact and sustained positive change.

At the Centre, we have been privy to sexual violence incidents and as first responders of some sort, I reiterate that sexual violence, sexual harassment, intimidate and victimization of girls and women in a school environment triggers emotions of anxiety, fear, disappointment and abandonment on the part of survivors. None of these emotions have the capability to enhance learning, critical thinking and assimilation for those experiencing them. Instead, the survivors are striped of confidence and the mental stability required for qualitative learning. This affects them in the present and in the future has far wider consequences for their future, with work and in building personal and professional relationships, a very important fiber of every society.

Fortunately, this webinar and the fortification of the justice system through the passage of the Anti-Sexual Harassment Bill signifies that Nigeria and our institutions are ready to take on the task of protecting our female students from sexual predators. I am optimistic that going forward, women will have better and safer learning experiences through our joint efforts and for a more prosperous society and country. I also appreciate the organizers and coordinators of the program lead by the Vice Chancellor Prof Eyitope Ogunbodede, and to all participants we are thankful for your presence and attendance and I wish us all a successful fight towards a most noble cause- a society where women do not have to live in terror but thrive in and out of formal learning environments.

A WINDOW OF OPPORTUNITY

STEVE ORONSAYE

Former Head of the Civil Sevice of the Federation makes suggestion on how
to engage the House of Representatives on the Bill already passed by the Senate

Let me begin by thanking the organizers of this Webinar. My intervention will be brief. I agree with the suggestions put forward by Ifueko (Okauru). However, because amendment of laws could be cumbersome, I suggest that we take the pragmatic approach. From the disclosure made by the Deputy Senate President, the Senate has concluded work on its version of the Bill with its passage. Since the House of Representatives is yet to conclude, perhaps we could consider the outcome of this Webinar as inputs for them for the Bill under consideration. We can look at the gaps, if any, in the Senate version, identify areas of intervention and then take to the House of Representatives for its consideration on a clause-by-clause basis. If the suggestions are already there, we can amend the clauses to make them more comprehensive. If not present, we should consider their possible inclusion as new clauses. With that, the House of Representatives can pass its version and proceed to the conference of both houses with its document. When the two houses come together at conference, the Senate should be persuaded to adopt the version passed by the House of Representatives, which now becomes the harmonized version to be taken back to the respective houses for passage.

ALL OFFENDERS MUST
FACE JUSTICE

ADEYINKA OLUMIDE-FUSIKA

Ife alumnus and Senior Advocate of Nigeria seeks expansion of the law on
sexual harassment to include work places

Mine is an observation regarding the Bill that the Deputy Senate President, Senator Ovie Omo-Agege, spoke about in his keynote address. By its long description, it is "A BILL FOR AN ACT TO PREVENT, PROHIBIT AND REDRESS SEXUAL HARASSMENT OF STUDENTS IN TERTIARY EDUCATIONAL INSTITUTIONS AND FOR OTHER MATTERS CONNECTED THEREWITH". Its objective, as stated in its proposed Section 1, is "… *to promote and protect ethical standards in tertiary education, the sanctity of the student-educator fiduciary relationship of authority, dependency and trust and respect for human dignity in tertiary educational institutions …*"

Just recently, the Federal High Court sentenced a dismissed a Professor Richard Akindele, now formerly of this University, to two-year imprisonment for offences bothering on sexual

179

harassment of a female student. The I.C.P.C. prosecuted the case under the provisions of an existing Act. What this tells us, as the Vice President, Prof. Yemi Osinbajo, SAN, mentioned in his own keynote address, is that it is not entirely true that we have been helpless to bring perpetrators to book because our existing laws did not contain provisions applicable to sexual harassment. What is closer to the truth is that there has, before now, been low awareness of the malaise, and those that have the responsibility of preventing and bringing perpetrators to justice have not also considered or taken it as one of their priorities. Happily, this is now changing.

On a personal note I remember that my own wife, Feyisikemi (Nee Egunjobi), now late, who graduated with a B.Sc. (Hons.) from this University in the late '80s suffered the same thing in the hands of one of her lecturers. Complaint to the departmental and faculty authorities were treated with complete nonchalance. It took the intervention of the Students Union to eventually save her from the randy lecturer. The Students Union was independent, strong and alive to its responsibilities in those days. University Administrators at the time saw and treated the institution of Student unionism as a key element of the University system. The lesson is that while an individual student stands little chance against his or her harasser who is a person in a position of authority over him or her, the equation becomes a little bit more balanced when the body of students, the Students Union, is well and alive to take up her battle. The Nigerian State and our University Administrators would therefore do well to change their intolerant attitude which has destroyed and rendered that institution unfit for purpose.

My other observation is that if we want to now make a law that is subject-specific to sexual harassment, rather than leaving it to existing general laws that prohibit and punish criminal behaviour, then the Bill should be such that can be applied to sexual harassment and sexual offences wherever and by whosoever committed. The Bill, as it currently stands is of restrictive application to "harassment of students in tertiary educational institutions". But it is not only students that can be victims of sexual harassment, and it is not only in tertiary institutions that it occurs. It happens also in workplaces, including mosques and churches, Nollywood and even the National Assembly. It will be tedious and unproductive to make separate laws to specifically apply to each place. I will therefore suggest that it be one of the outcomes or resolutions of this Webinar that the National Assembly revisit the Bill to address the observed weakness.

Sometimes classes run from 5pm to 8pm. I am more at risk leaving university at that time, but it's seen as my problem, not the university's. Girls don't really have support. If I say this [about abuse], who is going to defend me? The lecturer is in a good position. Schools are not willing to let go of lecturers for one of their students. Lecturers have the advantage.

– AMANDA DOTEH,
graduate of the University of Liberia

WHY LAWS ARE NOT ENOUGH

OKEY IKECHUKWU, mni

The Executive Director, Development Specs academy, Abuja, says that
stakeholders must go beyond laws to tackle the challenge

My suggestion this morning will be that this discussion
be further expanded on a later date, to include a wider cache
of concerned stakeholders. In this regard the Vice Chancellor
may wish to later convene a roundtable, made up of Deans of
Faculty, Heads of department and all Student leaders, including
students Hall Chairpersons. Only such a drill-down will bring
the lessons home and make this effort work in a lasting manner.
That is just a suggestion.

The other thing, of course, is only an observation. From the
attendance and list of participants on this topical issue, it would
seem that we've been speaking mostly to the converted. This
fact imposes on the university and the organizers involved the
additional unfinished business of rallying still more people,
including all lecturers and parents, for another engagement.
Our university teachers must really assume the role assigned to
them in Loco parentis and deliver value for our young people.

Finally, yes we are talking about laws to enforce the rights of victims, while restraining offenders. Laws are wonderful in this matter, but laws are not enough. The issues are way too serious just be restricted to laws lawmakers and the academia. I am sure some of us here know, as widely reported, that some of our law makers and public officials are routinely provided young people of the opposite gender as part of their menu, when they are out of their stations of primary official assignments. Is this true, or not? So, let us not pussyfoot on this matter. The challenge goes far across the wider society, so let us not carry on as if the academia should be the only platform under scrutiny on the issues before us.

Speaking from experience here, I once went on an official trip in 2001 to represent my boss, the then Minister of Transport, at a youth event in the University of Benin. It turned out later, as the evening was drawing to a close, that the student leadership of the host department had concluded arrangements to give me what I later learnt was called "kola" for the night. In declining the offer of kola (without the traditional "nut") I demanded to know why I was not even consulted on the mattet! Speechless, infuriated and really dumbfounded I wanted to know what in the world was going on. Now it was their turn to look at me with surprise. Then one of them ventured forward with an explanation he thought would put my mind at rest. "Oh sir, we only deal with responsible girls. For instance, the person we have in mind is one of our class mates. We know her very well."

Now, ladies and gentlemen, look at the concept the young man, a student in the university, was using: "these are responsible girls." What's the meaning of "responsible" in this context? From this short narrative, it should be clear that there is a thriving "industry" that needs to be dismantled across several frontiers. So I really thank Segun for his book. The problem is a national, for which a campaign that must be taken beyond the academia has become necessary.

CHAPTER NINE

LET'S MOVE FROM
PROMISES TO ACTION

BISI ADELEYE-FAYEMI

First Lady of Ekiti State and an Ife alumnus speaks on four key interventions
that stakeholders need to make

In the foreword I did for Olusegun Adeniyi's book, 'Naked Abuse', I shared an anecdote which speaks to how I first understood this issue as a student at the then University of Ife, now OAU, in the 1980s. The student whose story I told was both frustrated and devastated. She had become dehumanised.

Back then, hers was a cautionary tale on what happened if you spoke up about sexual harassment. That was how we got to understand the implications of sexual harassment on girls like us in the universities at the time. If something like that happened to you, there was no one to tell. If you tried to talk, the system had a way to punish you. That was a long time ago but the narrative itself has not changed. We still live in times when male teachers see female students as their fringe benefits and we still have a lot of young women living and suffering in silence.

This is 2020, exactly 25 years after some of us attended the Beijing Conference. As one of the young women who went to Beijing and who dreamt of a world where women would have full equal rights, a world in which women would be treated with dignity and respect, I am sad that we are far from being there. This is 25 years after, and I am still here on this Webinar, having a conversation about the dignity and rights of women.

This morning I would like to talk about moving from promises to action. This issue has been spoken about over and over again and certain promises have been made through the legal frameworks that have been put in place like the Violence Against Persons (Prohibition) Act; the Sexual Harassment Bill that the Senate has just passed and that is going to the House of Representatives and through OAU itself having a sexual harassment policy. I am aware that a couple of other universities like the University of Ibadan, Ekiti State University, Tai Solarin University of Education, also have their own Sexual Harassment and GBV Policies.

These are extremely important but they remain promises to women: that they are going to be heard, that they will be safe, that they will be protected. So, for me, the key question is, how can we move from those promises to action? How can we make these frameworks, these legislations that we have in place, these agreements, these codes of conduct, how can it mean something in the lives of ordinary female students who just want to go to school to get an education?

I want to talk about four key things. First, I believe that all our tertiary institutions need to demonstrate enough political will to show that they will not condone any form of violations against female students, that they will uphold the dignity and rights of both male and female students as well as the rights of all the teachers. This political will can be expressed for example, through how seriously the university takes issues around sexual abuse, sexual misconduct, sexual violence and related matters. It can also be reflected in terms of how many women are in leadership positions in the university because if we don't have enough women in critical places, this issue tends to get pushed to the margins. We have a Centre for Gender and Social Policy Studies at OAU which by the way we are extremely proud of, but we will also like to know for example, how much has the university itself internalised all these issues for it to mean something in terms of implementation? Political will is very important and added to that is the issue of resources - financial, material, technical and human resources that will be required to ensure that all these robust policies are actually implemented.

The second issue I want to address is that of legal and policy frameworks. We should think beyond the Sexual Harassment and GBV Policies within the university or what has just been passed at the National Assembly. The VAPP Act is an extremely important tool in addressing violations against women, and men as well, in the holistic sense. Sexual harassment is just one of many violations that we are talking about. I recommend that OAU work with the Osun State government. Osun State has a GBV Law and they have domesticated the VAPP Act. In every state where we have the domestication of the VAPP Act, there is a Gender Based Violence (GBV) Coordinating Mechanism and I believe that OAU needs to be represented on the equivalent of that mechanism in Osun State. In Ekiti State, for example, where we have a GBV law, we have an implementation mechanism and Ekiti State University is represented. I Chair that committee and we always insist that we need to hear the voices of tertiary institutions since a lot of cases of sexual violence and harassment happen there.

The third point I will like to make is around ownership of these issues. Community ownership, ownership by university authorities, ownership by the student bodies, ownership by everyone concerned - male and female, and that ownership can be expressed in different ways. For example, already we have heard about WARSHE which means Women against Rape, Sexual Harassment and Exploitation established by OAU lecturers to support their community around these issues. An organisation like WARSHE needs to be strengthened and supported and everyone needs to see themselves as critical stakeholders in the work that WARSHE does, in terms of providing critical services to students and faculties around sexual harassment and sexual violence.

Beyond that, I believe that every tertiary institution in Nigeria should have a Gender-Based Violence club. At OAU, I will like to see that we have a club on campus that is established to address the issue, and that has female and male members as well. It is important to involve men, like my brother, Olusegun Adeniyi, so they can begin to understand the implications of living in a patriarchal society and how a lot of men need to divest themselves of the privileges patriarchy confers on them, while women from a very early age need to understand how to survive life in deeply patriarchal communities.

Last but not the least, I will like to see more knowledge production and management. OAU is a leading university in Nigeria, one of the best in Africa. We need to see more research, more gender analysis, because I believe that gender analysis and teaching and study of gender issues are important. We seem to be losing our capacity for coherent feminist analysis, and the application of feminist tools. We cannot take a shower without getting wet. We cannot address gender-based violence or sexual harassment without addressing power dynamics and the inequalities between men and women. We have to process and understand how patriarchy affects every aspect of our lives.

I would therefore like to see more knowledge production, research, teaching and dissemination of information on these issues so that we can have the tools we need as we go about our work as policy makers, lecturers, practitioners, writers or students. Once again, I would like to thank the university and those who organised this webinar. I thank my brother, Olusegun Adeniyi for the wonderful work he has done on this issue. It is unfinished business. Gender equality and women empowerment are issues that we still need to continue to confront. We need to stop our society from treating women as second-class citizens because none of our development goals will be met if we continue to undermine women and girls and deprive them of qualitative education, which is a right and not a privilege.

Sexual harassment, sex for marks or marks for sex in universities is absolutely unacceptable.

– JANET KATAHA MUSEVENI,
Ugandan First Lady and Education Minister

CHAPTER TEN

THE IMPUNITY IS GETTING
OUT OF HANDS

JOY NGOZI EZEILO, (OON)

Professor of Public Law, University of Nigeria (UNN) and member, United
Nations Civil Society Advisory Board on Prevention of Sexual Exploitation and
Abuse says men and women must work together to fight the scourge

We are happy that men are are now involved in fighting the scourge of sexual violence against women. The support of men, especially in positions of power helps to amplify the voices of women. Sometimes it appears that women have not been doing anything to bring the issue of SH in the front burner of national discourse. But I tell you, women have been doing a lot. You will not believe that we had a camera ready, sexual harassment policy way back in 2007 and I involved critical stakeholders in developing this policy then, including the National Universities Commission (NUC), National Human Rights Commission and the Trade Unions. We had series of seminars, including at selected Universities. We produced a draft policy for educational and work places and the NUC forwarded to Universities but they said, 'oh, universities will look at it and adopt their separate policies.'

Today, we are all worried about the impunity. The spate of unwanted and unwarranted sexual advances and I had been dealing with this, both within the university and other academic institutions and with regard to work places. I recall one of the first public cases that I handled under my organization, WomenAid Collective (WACOL), it involved a girl working in a sports club. You know what sport club is. If you talk about sport club in Ibadan, Lagos or Enugu and she had the courage to come out and say 'this is what is happening to me. I'm being harassed by the secretary of the club and this is what it is leading to.' It finally went to court and before I knew it, there was a woman who was director who had to come all the way from her state to visit me and to meet with me because she was facing the situation of sexual harassment in her work place. I handled another involving a female employee at the Federal Ministry of Environment.

At some point WIMBIZ took it up and I was invited to speak in a seminar in 2006 in Lagos held at the Muson Shell Centre. It was an evening full packed programme with women in the corporate sector and from different parts of Nigeria gathered to discuss the ugly phenomenon of sexual harassment that they have experienced as students and then now, in work places, in the corporate sector. Women at that conference made it cleat that one out of any three successful women must have faced this sexual harassment in the course of her career. The burning question is why this epidemic? At WACOL, we have had cases and allegations of SH from staff of ministries and other private sectors. Some state panels had visited us but unfortunately sometimes nothing comes out of probes of those allegations. I have dealt with several cases in universities. There are some I handled in the universities and they have been very quick in response and taking urgent action to redress the situation, but it's not always that you get quick responses. Cases can drag thereby in case of tertiary institutions prolonging student's stay or causing some other unpleasant consequences.

So, when a dean and a professor and people in positions of power and authority exploit the vulnerability of students it saddens me and urgently begs for action to halt the impunity. It is this vexed issue of sexual harassment that is of growing concern that we are talking about and that has been well documented in the erudite work of Olusegun Adeniyi that covered case studies in 29 African countries, including Nigeria.

The issue is, how is our country responding to it? When I did a global study in 2007 it showed how it is being handled effectively in other jurisdictions. However, in the case of Nigeria, it looks like we take one step forward, and take 10 backward. Some people are trying to distract and trivialise current legislative attempt to criminalise sexual harassment by raising issues as to why winking should amount to SH. On a serious note, is it okay for a lecturer to wink to his student? It is gestural and when you are looking at the forms of sexual harassment, it could be physical harassment, kissing, parting, pinching, touching. The gestural definitely includes winking.

I will tell you my experience as a law student and the incident happened in my final year student, I had actually gotten married, and I was in this lecturer's office that took us on tutorial to pass my quiz and on coming in, this lecturer just grabbed to kiss me. I was pregnant and I pushed the lecturer hard and left his office. I immediately came out and told my friend what just transpired. I'm not a student that needed help to pass as I never got anything less than B grade in all my law courses. Some students, are first class students but reducing your grade just because you didn't comply with unwanted sexual advances make them to lose something and this very painful. Verbal harassment is also part of it. Gestural harassment making gestures with hands, with fingers, with legs, they should form part of it and people shouldn't be surprised that this is in the Bill. It is not okay to wink at your student because as a lecturer you're in in locus parenting and supposed to guide your students morally and academically. Again, the vice-president spoke about the abuse of power and the corruption in it, which is true and I think the other aspect we need to know is that it is a form of sex discrimination that happens to women because of their gender.

A situation of this for that- quid pro quo- if you don't give me this, you won't get this create a hostile educational environment, that is why we are talking of safe places and ending the impunity, which obviously requires a collective and concerted action. Some institutions will not take proactive measure or treat positive cases until it gets to social media and becomes embarrassing, 'oh, okay, it's about cold room now at UNILAG.' It's about OAU today. Tomorrow, it's may be about any other University. Once it goes quiet, I tell you, nothing happens and victims may never get justice.

I commend OAU particularly for taking the action that we saw. But I don't know about the victim now, whether the victim herself feels that justice has been done in her case and this is very important that we don't forget because I have seen cases that I handled personally, and as soon as they take action, in fact, there is one that I am handling currently and as soon as she comes, 'VC will take action. Others will take action,' and before you know it, some people will go to the back, 'let this woman not be involved,' because they know you, your capacity and what you cannot tolerate, especially corruption or impunity of this sort.

As a dean, I read before my colleagues a zero-tolerance

approach that is how to raise accountability stake. University administrators must show leadership and determination to expose perpetrators. We must build student's confidence because the students don't really trust the system because once they report, they bring themselves out, and if nothing happens you can imagine the risk and the discomfort they may suffer. Thus, we must get the process right and importantly adopt victim centred-approach. The student must be involved in any investigating body or committee and they must take centre stage in any decision affecting them. There is need for whistle-blower's protection and we must broaden the scope and not just think that SH is limited to student-lecturer. It's usually the major one - lecturer-student, but there is also student vs. student, there is lecturer-student, there is also student and other university staff, including administration staff. All categories should worry us but the one that is most worrisome of them all, is, I have seen cases where students, maybe class rep procures other female students for a particular lecturer and they do this and they are part of the system. It's just like pimping fellow students. If you want this mark...That is why It's sex for grade. It's extortion and that is a form of sexual harassment. It's unwanted, serious and it demeans a woman, humiliates and creates a hostile intimidating environment.

I want to say that in dealing with this problem because our laws, have never been so explicit, whether it is criminal law or other laws on this issue and I know that it is a matter in which every state has the right to make its legislation or law. If it is the federal law, the bill eventually is going to be limited to FCT. Every other state has to get on board and beyond the state, every institution of higher learning need to also have a law in their criminal justice system that can be used to prosecute, but it's not always easy even to succeed.

I think in offering a recommendation, going forward, I thank OAU for hosting this webinar and I think it's something that every university, every institution must do and let us not delude ourselves that this is just happening in the University, the cankerworm has spread to all levels of education so secondary school level is also seriously affected. Our value system has been so corrupted and skewed that some do not even appreciate that what they are doing is wrong. Some young male lecturers think is okay because they are not married to befriend their students in intimate ways. That's amount to conflict of interest i.e. in case you have a consensual relationship with your student. You have to declare it and then nothing concerning her will come to you. You cannot also teach her. You cannot grade her. You cannot mark her scripts and I think that is fact is also lost on us and there is need to clarify this in a code of conduct or ethics to be adopted by institutions of higher learnings.

First, there has to be adoption of sexual harassment policy at all levels of education. This is very important. Legislative initiative is already on. That is why I say it takes a collective, you see action from executive, from legislature and the judiciary. In fact, decisions of court enforcing extant laws will encourage report and wide mass media coverage will help prevent this ugly phenomenon of SH. That is why I'm appreciating the book of Segun Adeniyi on SH. It cannot be pushed underground and ASUU cannot be put on the defensive. They should actually be proactive in finding a solution to the menace.

The management and administrative sector within the educational institution needs to put in place an effective committee to deal with the menace. We have to put people of integrity in the committee. There are people you put within the committee; they will kill the work. They will be too slow. The student will not get justice. If somebody that is supervising a student in final year, for instance, counting her days, is sexually harassing her and you are talking of changing supervisor, and you have a committee that will sit for months, what justice will that person get? And it comes back to justice delayed is justice denied. It has to be one that is quick.

As out federal lawmakers are dealing with it, we need to get to the state level. They have to do it with proper definition and procedure to include in our penal laws on the subject, providing in clear terms, what amounts to sexual harassment. What does it mean? What we have now is not very precise. It's not very clear and basically inadequate to meet the high incidents of varying dimensional of sexual harassment. But when we have a law that falls into crime, it's very important that we know how to act as Universities. When it becomes a crime now, they cannot say, it is a crime, we cannot deal with it. It's a crime, let's call police. The university has to take prompt administrative action that will protect the student and discipline erring employee of the University found wanting.

So, we should know that it is important to give examples of relationships that may constitute sexual harassment because truly, some people don't know, like when they think they are unmarried and they can harass and invite their students to their beds. There should be a clear prohibition. There shouldn't be any student meeting in lecturers' homes, in their hotel rooms and other places outside the university for supervision or if even after work.

I know students have ended up being married by lecturers. We are not saying it is a bad idea, but you must be clear that you cannot have anything to do with the student. Dissemination of the policy, reporting in confidentiality, informal resolution procedure and the issue of also the penalty for wrong accusation, all of that should be part of policies on SH for tertiary educational institutions.

I support an initiative that would require every lecturer to sign a code of ethics which includes a clear declaration of zero tolerance for sexual harassment. Educational institutions should be at the frontline of the battle to combat all vices in impeding safe learning environment, particularly sexual harassment, sorting and cultism. This has a devastating effect on learning and impacts overall on quality of education and certificates acquired therefrom.

CHAPTER ELEVEN

RESTORING THE DIGNITY
OF WOMEN

SAUDATU MAHDI

The Secretary General of Women's Rights Advancement and Protection
Alternative, (WRAPA) argues for the restoration of the dignity of women

For many years, one issue that all the frontline NGOs
have been speaking to is the issue of the woman - her right
to dignity, her right to protection through advocacy and her
attitude to as well as the voice and agency for her to speak up
when her rights are abused or stand threatened as in the saga
of sex for grade in our educational institutions.

Having listened to the previous speakers, let me dwell on
probably the issue we have not addressed our minds to. A lot
of parents find themselves in the paradox of their daughters
coming home to complain of carrying over, to complain of
suffering the syndrome of course change. For a lot of these
daughters, a profile for instability and insecurity emerges. So,
I said let me look at what we don't probably pay attention to

which is the issue of breach of trust. I ask if lecturers, students, parents and institutional administrators see the big picture of abuse of trust?

The foundation for the relationship between a teacher and student or an educator and recipient is one that is first of all built on trust. It is based on the principles of trust, and the principles of power dynamics in trusted relationships. In this instance accessing safe education is the challenge. What is in for the teacher, or university lecturer? For the lecturer, what you have is a status of co-parenting, which then puts on that person a duty of trust and care. It also gives that lecturer the power of knowledge and moral authority.

Then, there is the issue of responsibility. In days gone by, in schools, and in a bid for safety and protection you found parents attaching children, especially girls; college fathers/ mothers, you found mentors, you found guardians amongst teachers and other school employees. Sometimes, you are taken to an environment where you have nobody and your teacher is made your guardian; and that places a responsibility, a duty on that person.

On the other side, this student who sees trust as the fundamental of the relationship, feels a sense of security and dependency. That female child/student is then dependent on the whims and caprices of that responsible or that compromised lecturer/teacher. In that context you may have on her side, a situation of desperation. Desperation erodes trust and jeopardises safety.

That desperation gives room for the child or for the female student in this instance, to do anything to get what she desires to either complete her course or move forward in life. That trust deficit and what it procures bring isolation and self blame for consequencies in her study, dignity, and safety. She sees herself as probably the only person who is not making progress because she didn't do what the lecturer asked her to do. She is isolated and broken because she cannot speak to any other person. Her parents who sent her on a trust and safety ticket through university structures, through a lecturer and through a system are hard put to see the breach of trust.

Worst of all, she is surrounded by a weak support system that does not protect or assure her. Not knowing she is not the only one; not knowing there are people out there who will support her; and not knowing there are legal frameworks that can work for her; she is stranded. For all she cares, she finds herself standing alone without any support. The breach of trust in the lecturer, who is a co-parent as our Vice-President said earlier, destroys the locus parenting status and devastates this child. I continue to say in all incidents of sexual and grade transactions trust is gone through the window. Because they trust, many parents and society indeed are not willing to listen or understand. This makes her more vulnerable losing capacity to even rationalise what her life around her is all about. It erodes her human dignity and just as we said earlier the fact that it is an enterprise needed to give her a start in life; she is faced with confusion and the threat of the loss of her chance to attain her aspirations or life potentials.

It limits and forces her choices to say okay, I don't need to trust. All I need is what I can do with my body. It's my body I can give out first and justify later. That transaction alone is in itself dehumanising. The story from Erelu about the girl who tried to undress herself and calling out on her lecturer tells you her desperation level and the fact that she had descended to the level where her only outlet was to do what he asked of her.

Either, he had not had the courage to rape her; or probably because she had not given him the opportunity of being in his office. This speaks to the notion of faulty location. Again it begins to put a woman or a female candidate, a female student into some state of self-incrimination and enquiry. 'Is it that I don't do the right thing by going to the right places?' Again that puts down her capacity to stand up to that lecturer and say NO.

In all of what I have said, I find two major points, which I will like us to bear in mind as we speak to this issue. That parents send their daughters to school for any form of education placing a responsibility for safety in the environment of learning. That safety is the responsibility of the institutional administrators and the actors that are saddled with that trust. The second thing I will like to place on the table is that female students, whose trust is abused, need to be empowered. They need voice and agency and what WASH, WRAPA, WACOL, WARDC and all other NGOs are doing is to see that they empower the girls/survivors such that they have capacity to recognise that human dignity is inalienable and not negotiable; and that education is a right and not a privilege.

That the ability to push back, to say NO, is rooted in their safety and in their survival. First, they need to organise and they need to be supported to defend that human dignity by pushing back on their aggressors be them lecturers, administrative staff, or fellow students.

On the side of the institutions, what are those safety measures that we can put in place so that we consolidate trust and ensure that trust plays out in favour of the female child. Many suggestions have been made. Technology has been put forward. CCTV is expensive but it is probably the only thing, although we have seen in many instances of people who cover up and do what they want. Suggestions have also been made in the book by my brother, Segun Adeniyi, on anonymity on exam scripts; about medical and psychological support for these young girls.

We have also seen experiences from other climes where modes and hours for consultations are defined and everybody is made to comply with them. Doing that will consolidate on the trust responsibility of the institutions and especially where we have safe guarding protocols that students understand, that lecturers understand and that all comply with.

Safeguarding the trust that has been placed on all in the education system by parents of female daughters is a duty, and a moral obligation to discharge

My conclusion, ladies and gentlemen, is that the incidence of sex for grade transactions is only a pointer of an underlying larger problem. Here I am agreeing with Don Brown, American author & Attorney when he posits: 'An incident (sex 4 Grades in this instance) is just the tip of the iceberg, a sign of a much larger problem below the surface'

This problem as said by the last two speakers is about the human dignity of the woman. It is about her right to education to achieve her full potential. It is also about her right to be protected by state, family and institutions. It is also about putting down impunity of transactional learning in our tertiary institutions. It is also about being able to support and establish systems that consolidate trust, support female students in universities, in secondary schools and everywhere to speak up and demand for justice.

Let's be clear: Sexual violence – any form of violence – is simply violence. There is no excuse. There is no justification. And there must be zero tolerance. All of us must stand up and speak out. Let's stand with our mothers, our sisters, our daughters, our partners.

– AMINA J. MOHAMMED,
Deputy Secretary General of the United Nations

WHY MEN'S VOICES
ALSO MATTER

*Against the background of the campaign that being the victims, the
issue of sex for grades should be left to female writers, I spoke at
the Ife Webinar on why it would take all critical voices, male and
female, joining in the conversation to to catalyse normative change.*

In writing my book, 'From Frying Pan to Fire: How
African Migrants Risk Everything in their Futile Search for
a Better Life in Europe' published in 2018, I visited many
cities in Italy, Spain and the United Kingdom. But it was on
the continent (of Africa) that I was confronted with perhaps
the worst instances of those emblems of shame for which
our country is fast becoming notorious. In an International
Organisation for Migration (IOM) centre housing trafficked
under-aged girls in Bamako, the Malian capital, I met
a Nigerian girl who shared with me her pathetic story of
how she was cajoled to abandon secondary school by the
sister of a friend who promised to take her abroad where she
could earn big money working in a salon. And, as it so often
happens, the story ended in Djinja Kayes, Southwest Mali,
where she was sold to a notorious Nigerian 'Madam' who

immediately forced the young girl into prostitution after subjecting her to a ritual oath.

In that book, I interrogated the desperation that made so many of our young citizens embark on perilous journeys that most often ended in the Sahara Desert, or on the Mediterranean Sea. But my experience in Mali opened my eyes to the vexatious issue of how vulnerable young women spend the prime of their lives satiating the pleasures of men and women who enslave and rob them of self-autonomy. I also encountered this phenomenon in Benin, the Edo State capital in Nigeria, where I spent considerable time interrogating the Italian connections that facilitate trafficking these women. I included a chapter on my investigations titled 'Edo and the Prostitution Ring' in the book, and I have written several columns on the issue since then. My experience led me to ponder the plight of women and girls in Nigeria more generally.

Writing 'From Frying Pan to Fire' left me with the uncomfortable realization that much of human trafficking and irregular migration, and perhaps so many other ills in our society, are underpinned by sexual violence. I also came to the conclusion that this is a societal problem and it is going to take all of society to solve it. However, for any intervention to be effective, it must deal with both the demand and supply side of the problem. Therefore, following the scandal involving Professor Richard Akindele and a female graduate student, Monica Osagie, at my alma mater, Obafemi Awolowo University, and at the Faculty of Administration from where I graduated, I saw sex for grades on our campuses as another dangerous dimension of the same malaise. And it occurred to me that to catalyse normative change, it would take all critical voices, male and female, joining in the conversation.

I am strongly persuaded that it is only when we succeed in curbing predatory behaviour on our campuses that we can truly begin to make education spaces safe for women and girls in our country and on our continent. However, in writing the book, I benefited from insights provided by respected female voices who are outspoken on the issue, including some that are here today. At the end, the use of two paragraphs from an online public statement at the back page of the book turned out to be a problem that generated social media storm. The position of the African Feminist Initiative (AFI), which I accept, is that use of a part of their public statement as a blurb for the book and listing their names without seeking prior permission, undermined the concept of consent which is at the heart of the issue dealt with in the book. The good thing is, I learned some important lessons from that regrettable experience. The many interactions that followed the publication and the choices I eventually made, led me to choose this topic.

Student-teacher relationships have facilitated an environment for unwholesome practices on university campuses across the continent and this sustains my conviction that writing 'NAKED ABUSE: Sex for Grades in African Universities' was worth the effort. My decision to embark on the project does not detract from the fact that she who feels it knows it, and it was never my intention to usurp women's voices as some of my critics claimed. I understand that in this battle, women can speak for themselves. Not only are they doing so clearly, the rest of the society is finally paying attention. I agree with some critics that this is not an area where men "have a starring role," but insisting on dichotomizing voices that can advocate for better social practices is not helpful in the long run. Everyone who has a conscience should raise their voice on this salient social issue in order to be counted. If men should reduce sexual violence, especially in institutions of high learning in Nigeria and across Africa to a "women's issue" and sit back, they are just as morally complicit.

Meanwhile, I understand those who argue that a dialogue that reflects their unique perspectives and values should be left to peers. For so long, women have been excluded from important conversations, including those directly affecting them. But considering that sexual violence is a symptom of a society that has allowed sexism and other forms of inequality to fester, the issue at stake is an ethical one. The burden of uplifting our society can therefore not be reduced to "women's problem" and men conveniently shut up. It will take a collaborative effort of all critical stakeholders to rid the society of the problem in all its manifestations. And every voice counts.

If we agree that it is society that is harmed by transactional sex on our campuses, then it would be counterproductive to restrict those who should engage on the subject because the perpetrators of the violence can hide under the silence of their fellow men. No voice, whether that of an individual or a collective, should be discounted if we are going to put an end to what has become "entrenched notions of control and entitlement."

Fortunately, this point is being increasingly made by stakeholders: From Gloria Steinem, respected American journalist and activist who has for the past five decades championed women's cause and is generally regarded as the 'Mother of Feminism' to Julia Gillard, former Australian Prime Minister and leader of the Labour party from 2010 to 2013. Men, according to Gillard, have a critical role to play in gender issues. While admitting that there is still a long way to go before there is a universal acceptance of equality of gender and that one should not oppress the other in any way or form, Gillard, who currently chairs the Global Institute for Women's Leadership, argues that, "we'll only get there by drawing more men into the conversation."

Here, let me make it clear. In this kind of conversation, it is important to reiterate that asking men to speak up is not tantamount to asking them to supplant women. What I advocate is for men to use the privilege that patriarchal society has afforded them to stand up to the same structures of power. As men, we cannot afford silence. We can use our voices to reinforce the argument advanced by feminist advocates. After all, we are stakeholders too. We have mothers, wives, and daughters who are affected by this issue one way or the other, and we have a moral duty to stand up for them. The International Centre for Research on Women (ICRW) could not have been more apt when it says that a campaign like this works better when everyone plays since "both women and men live within patriarchal power structures, uphold those structures, are concerned by those structures, and are responsible for transforming them."

In my book, I referenced Prof Oluyemisi Obilade whom I am meeting for the first time today, albeit virtually. She argued that not a few male lecturers see their female student as 'fringe benefits' and that, for me, is another reason men should challenge their peers on entrenched bad behavior. Incidentally, shortly after my book went to press, a friend visited my office and while discussing the issue of sex for grades, he shared with me a story which confirmed Prof Obilade's thesis. In the course of his visit to a town in the South-west where a federal university is located, according to his account, a lecturer-friend visited his hotel and reportedly told him: "I will send one of my female students to keep you company for the night. Since our pay is meagre, that is the only 'fringe benefit' we enjoy on this job." That mentality is wrong on all counts.

When a university lecturer readily pimps female students to male friends as the aforementioned instance demonstrated, it must mean that he 'rewards' those exploited female students with inflated grades. There are two crimes he is committing: sexual exploitation and the debasement of knowledge. Since both harm the individuals (whose worth and the credentials they parade are diminished) and the larger society (left with certificated illiterates), ridding our campuses of such irresponsible male lecturers is critical. That is why peer to peer interventions should not be seen as encroachment on anyone's turf. It is a collective moral responsibility.

The challenge, as Obilade also recounted, is compounded by the fact that in most instances, there are no avenues for seeking redress that students can access without compounding the harm being done to them. She cited cases of female students who would complain to their head of department about lecturers harassing them and the response they would get is: 'Give him what he wants.'

What that suggests is an ingrained culture, and that is why interventions from men are likely to receive more traction. Taking advantage of the platforms that some of us have will definitely not hurt. Besides, as men, we can frame the narrative in a way that catches the attention of men, by looking at all sides, including those that women may find 'offensive' even when it is real. For instance, a chapter in 'NAKED ABUSE' addresses the 'other side of the coin' argument that men often make when it comes to sexual harassment and demonstrates that looking at the issue does not necessarily absolve perpetrators of accountability. The argument is that there are women and girls whose philosophy is to 'use what they have to get what they want'. On university campuses, those kind of girls 'willingly' offer their bodies to lecturers in exchange for grades. It is important to address these kinds of argument, as I did in 'NAKED ABUSE', if we are to break down social resistance to gender equity.

Men's voices are also important because they can reinforce that this is not an 'us versus them' situation that often necessitates unhelpful pushback. Men can amplify voices of the victims, contribute to holding an oppressive system accountable and put the message in places where the voices of women are discounted for the time being. From my experience, in using our voices, men can also unlearn some of the cultural gender discrimination we may not even be aware of.

The key issues in the phenomenon of sex for grades is the misuse of power and privilege on the one hand and abuse of trust on the other. But the problem is being reinforced by inequities that are "rooted in uneven dynamics that give disproportionate power to one group versus another", and because of that, according to Laura Amaya, Clare Schroder, Sandra Medrano and Alexandra Geertz in their joint paper on why men must be drawn to the conversation, "Irrespective of the amount we invest in women, men also need to be willing participants in the redistribution of power between genders."

I am well aware that when it comes to sex for grades on our campuses, one cannot canvass the argument of power redistribution since it is between the teacher and the learner but we can insist that such power be exercised with a high degree of responsibility.

When we were putting this programme together, I told the Vice Chancellor that I am more interested in listening to the views of our women, which is why we carefully selected the panel. I have certainly learnt a lot in recent weeks about gender. And some of the people here today are my teachers. Bisi Adeleye-Fayemi, Saudatu Mahdi, Joy Ezeilo and many others that are not here, like Oby Ezekwesili, Ayisha Osori, Bimbola Adelakun, Chioma Agwuegbo, Ifueko Omoigui-Okauru, Molara Wood, Maryam Uwais, Ifioma Malo, Yemi Adamolekun, Ayo Obe, Ndidi Nwuneli, Hadiza El-Rufai, Ngozi Azodoh, Jackie Farris. These are some of the voices I shall always listen to in these matters.

As I keep telling them, since we men are seen as part of the problem, it will not hurt if we are also part of the solution. Our joint endeavour today is therefore to begin a conversation on how we can find that solution, for the greater good of our beloved country. And continent!

Printed in Great Britain
by Amazon

27004094R00128